DANIEL HAGADORN

Preparing Kids for LIFE

REAL HOPE
FOR SPECIAL NEEDS FAMILIES

www.PK4L.com

How The Brain Works
& Why That's Great News
For Your Kids

Real Hope For Special Needs Families: How The Brain Works & Why That's Great News For Your Kids

PK4L Publishing
www.PK4L.com

Copyright © 2018 by Daniel M. Hagadorn

All rights reserved, including the right to reproduce this eBook or any portion thereof in any manner whatsoever. For more information, address:

Daniel Hagadorn
www.PK4L.com
dh@PK4L.com

Every attempt has been made to source all quotes properly.

Photo credits: Unsplash; Pixabay

ISBN: 978-0-9992827-2-4

10 9 8 7 6 5 4 3 2 1

First edition, 2018

Published in the United States of America

TABLE OF CONTENTS

INTRODUCTION: The problem. The symptoms. The hope.	1
STEP №1: Assess their nutritional intake	9
STEP №2: Assess their physical activity	13
STEP №3: Assess their social/emotional development	15
STEP №4: Assess your family time	17
TOOL №1: For your family life	21
TOOL №2: For your school life	23
TOOL №3: For your home life	25
RECOMMENDED RESOURCES: Dr. Robert Melillo	27
TABLE OF APPENDICES	29
APPENDIX 1: The Hemispheres Explained	31
APPENDIX 2: The Primitive Reflexes	43
APPENDIX 3: The Nutritional Guide	61
APPENDIX 4: The Activities Guide	73
APPENDIX 5: The Resource Guide	103

INTRODUCTION

The Way It Was

Families with special needs children were given little to no hope, and children were **routinely stamped with labels** that were…

- **Over-diagnosed** and **over-applied**.
- **Unhelpful** in understanding the problem or finding solutions.

UNTIL neuroscientists began to gain a better understanding of (1) how the brain works and (2) how the brain can improve.

The Growing Epidemic

Each year, an estimated 1.5 million children (1 out of 6) are diagnosed with autism, Asperger's syndrome, ADHD, dyslexia, or obsessive-compulsive disorder.

- According to a 2014 report published by the National Center for Learning Disabilities (NCLD), at least 5.7 million school-age children are affected by some form of learning disability.
  - It also found that approximately 4 to 7% had **both** a learning disability and ADHD.
- In 2015, childstats.gov reported that 42.2 million children ages 4-17 used special education services for either serious or minor emotional/behavioral problems.
- In 2015, the National Center for Education Statistics (NCES) reported that there were 6.6 million—or 13% of all public-school students—ages 3-21, who were receiving special education services.
  - Among that number, 35% had specific learning disabilities.

These numbers present several important questions…

INTRODUCTION

① What is the meaning of these diagnoses?

② Why has there been such a dramatic increase in neuro-behavioral disorders?

③ Can they be improved?

The debate over questions 1 and 2 will likely continue, but the answer to question 3 is a resounding "YES."

Just The Facts On Pharmaceuticals

This is a controversial subject with passions running high on both sides of the debate, but take a moment to consider the following from drugwatch.com:

According to *Health Care for America Now (HCAN)*, the world's eleven largest drug companies collectively recorded a profit of **$711.4 billion** between 2003 and 2012. In 2014, the global revenue for pharmaceuticals exceeded **$1 trillion** (cf. drugwatch.com).

In 2013, the trade group PhRMA employed 50+ current or former staff members who once served in the political arena, including:

- 36 who worked for a member of Congress.
- 13 who worked for a federal agency.
- 12 who worked for a congressional committee.
- 2 who worked for the White House.
- 1 who worked in the courts system.

Typically, to fully vaccinate a child through age 18...

- Requires 35 office visits that cumulatively cost $2,500 (+/-).
- In 2014, 4.4 million young men and women turned 18 = $11 billion worth of revenue just from vaccinations.

2014 data from the Federal Elections Commission (FEC) revealed that the Pharmaceuticals/Health Products Industry...

- Contributed $177.3 million to politicians and/or political campaigns.
- Employed 1,360 lobbyists.

INTRODUCTION

According to data released by the BBC from GlobalData, *9 of 10* Big Pharma companies spend more *marketing their drugs to consumers than they spend on research and development (R&D).*

- Ex.: Johnson & Johnson's marketing budget of $17.5 billion is 113% larger than the $8.2 billion it spent on R&D.
- Ex.: Pfizer's marketing budget of $11.4 billion is 137% larger than the $4.8 billion it spent on R&D.

The United States is *1 of only 2 countries in the world* where drug companies are allowed to market directly to consumers.

All journals are bought—or at least cleverly used—by the pharmaceutical industry.
—RICHARD SMITH
former editor of *British Medical Journal*

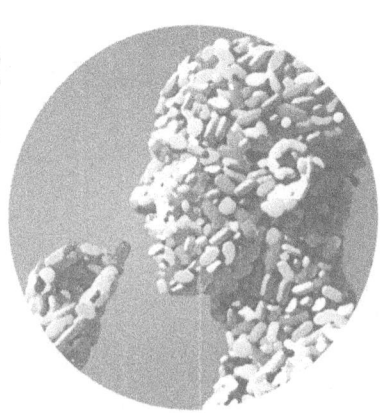

The Two Takeaways

① Pharmaceutical companies have made an enormous financial investment in (1) lobbying and (2) marketing to promote prescription medications and vaccinations.

② None of the above facts are necessarily good or bad, right or wrong...but DO need to be part of the conversation.

In the final analysis, everyone must do their own research and decide for themselves what motivates the pharmaceutical industry.

BUT...if husbands and wives have killed each other over $200,000 of life insurance money...isn't it worth at least asking what pharmaceutical executives would be willing to do in order to protect hundreds of BILLIONS of dollars of profit?

INTRODUCTION

How The "Problem" Is "Solved"

Learning disabilities are typically addressed…

With medications. Taking them "helps" the child to focus MORE which will then "help" them to achieve MORE.

With academics. Completing an ever-increasing AMOUNT of academic work will "help" the child to learn MORE.

With accommodations. Funneling the child through a continuum of services and modifications will "help" to compensate for their lack of progress.

Um…and putting gasoline on a fire will "help" it burn more, but is that really the point of all this? Are these "solutions" actually "helping" to solve anything?

THE NON-SOLUTION

The Actual Problem

An imbalance in brain activity between the right and left hemispheres. In fact, research has demonstrated that the brain literally becomes "desynchronized" as a result of "under-connectivity" (out of rhythm). However, when the foundational causes of Functional Disconnection Syndrome (FDS) are properly addressed, the brain improves.

…From de-synchronized to synchronized.
…From under-connected to connected.
…From imbalanced to balanced.

INTRODUCTION

FDS causes an anatomical imbalance (i.e., certain areas of the brain become physically larger or more mature than others).

- This imbalance is also found in electrical and metabolic activity and is accompanied by "an unevenness of skills characteristic of these disorders."
- Areas that cannot synchronize in space and time are unable to share information and do not develop connections (i.e., they appear under-connected).
- The most significant under-development/connection appears to be located in the corpus callosum (the area linking the two hemispheres).

IF there is no sign of any pathology, or physical injury to the brain (i.e., the MRI indicates "normal"), then "inflammatory changes are usually distributed equally."

- Consequently, this appears to indicate that the inflammation is a *result* of FDS, and NOT the cause.

Autism

Reduced activity and coherence in the right hemisphere "explains all symptoms of autistic spectrum disorder, as well as observed increases in sympathetic activation." However, IF the problem of autistic spectrum disorder is primarily the desynchronization and ineffective communication between the hemispheres, THEN the most effective way to address those symptoms is to improve coordination between areas of the brain.

- The BEST approach would include a "multimodal therapeutic model that combines somatosensory, cognitive, behavioral, and biochemical interventions."
- Each of these models will improve overall health, reduce inflammation, and increase right hemisphere activity until becoming temporally connected with the left hemisphere.
- Consequently, "increasing the baseline oscillation speed of one entire hemisphere improves the coordination/coherence between the two hemispheres and allows for improved motor-cognitive connection."

INTRODUCTION

In Other Words...

➡ One hemisphere of the brain develops faster than the other.
➡ The over-developed hemisphere compensates by trying to do the job of the under-developed hemisphere.
➡ Since that hemisphere of the brain was not designed to do those jobs, it performs them poorly.
➡ Compounding the problem, neither hemisphere communicates very well with the other.
➡ However, once the under-developed hemisphere becomes sufficiently developed through appropriate stimulation, both hemispheres can begin synchronizing (i.e., "communicating") with each other.
➡ Increased synchronization results in significant improvement...*emotionally, mentally, and physically.*

The Reason For Hope

Scientific research from the 1990s made four key discoveries...and the *hope these discoveries offer to children with FDS cannot be over-emphasized.*

① **Neuroplasticity.** This can occur throughout a person's life, which means that it is "never too late" to improve.
② **Invention of the MRI.** This allowed scientists to locate the parts of the brain that performed specific functions.
③ **Functions of the brain.** All human functions are distributed either on the right or left hemisphere of the brain.
④ **Functional Disconnection Syndrome (FDS).** The root cause of all developmental delays.

Additional research from the 1990s revealed...

- Stimulation and training can change the brain both physically and chemically.
- Brain cells can grow larger and the spaces between them can become smaller.
- Additional connections can be formed and activated, which increases the brain's processing speed.

INTRODUCTION

[NOTE: As a high school teacher since 2003, I have personally observed several young men and women who simply had strong or energetic personalities treated as though they had a learning disability. *While there ARE legitimate reasons for pharmaceutical intervention, there are ALSO several important factors to thoughtfully consider before using them.]*

How Does The Brain Change?

Harnessing the brain's neuroplasticity to promote beneficial change requires two things:

① The **exact stimuli** must be delivered in the **appropriate sequence** with **precise timing.**
② The **training** must be **intensive, repetitive,** and **progressively challenging.**

To achieve maxim improvement, the combination and timing of the stimuli is critical:

① The body must be physically stimulated to strengthen connectivity between the two hemispheres of the brain.
② AND to do that, the body requires appropriate nutrition and supplementation to support the development of the central nervous system and brain.
③ Customized academic stimulation is also needed to activate the under-developed hemisphere of the brain.
④ Consistent, specific exercises need to be performed to inhibit (and eventually eliminate) the primitive reflexes (which have an "expiration date").

> This is why we must do more than just "understand" the existing situation. Especially since the school system often compounds the problem by forcing teachers (who truly want to help their kids) apply unhelpful labels and use the wrong tools.

INTRODUCTION

notes

STEP №1
Assess their nutritional intake

Make A List

- ❏ Record the foods your child currently eats.
- ❏ Record the portion size.
- ❏ Record the number of times they eat every day.
- ❏ Record their reactions to the food (e.g., emotional, mental, physical).

Things To Consider Eliminating From Your Child's Diet

- ❏ **Dairy and gluten**

- ❏ **Fried Foods**

- ❏ **High Fructose Corn Syrup (HFCS)**
  - Read labels carefully as this can be alternatively labeled: maize syrup, glucose syrup, fructose syrup, tapioca syrup, dahlia syrup, fruit fructose, crystalline fructose, or isoglucose.
  - Basically, if the label doesn't say "sugar" or "cane sugar," it is almost certainly some form of HFCS.

- ❏ **False sugars ("diet" drinks, etc.)**
  - Ex.: artificial sweeteners like Acesulfame-K, Aspartame, Equal®, NutraSweet®, Saccharin, Sweet'n Low®, Sucralose, Splenda®, Sorbitol, et. al.

- ❏ **Artificial flavorings**
  - Benzoate preservatives (BHT, BHA, TBHQ)
  - Brominated vegetable oil (BVO)
  - MSG (Monosodium Glutamate)
  - Olestra®
  - Shortening and other hydrogenated/ partially hydrogenated oils
  - Sodium nitrite/nitrate

STEP №1: Assess their nutritional intake

Things To Consider Adding To Your Child's Diet...

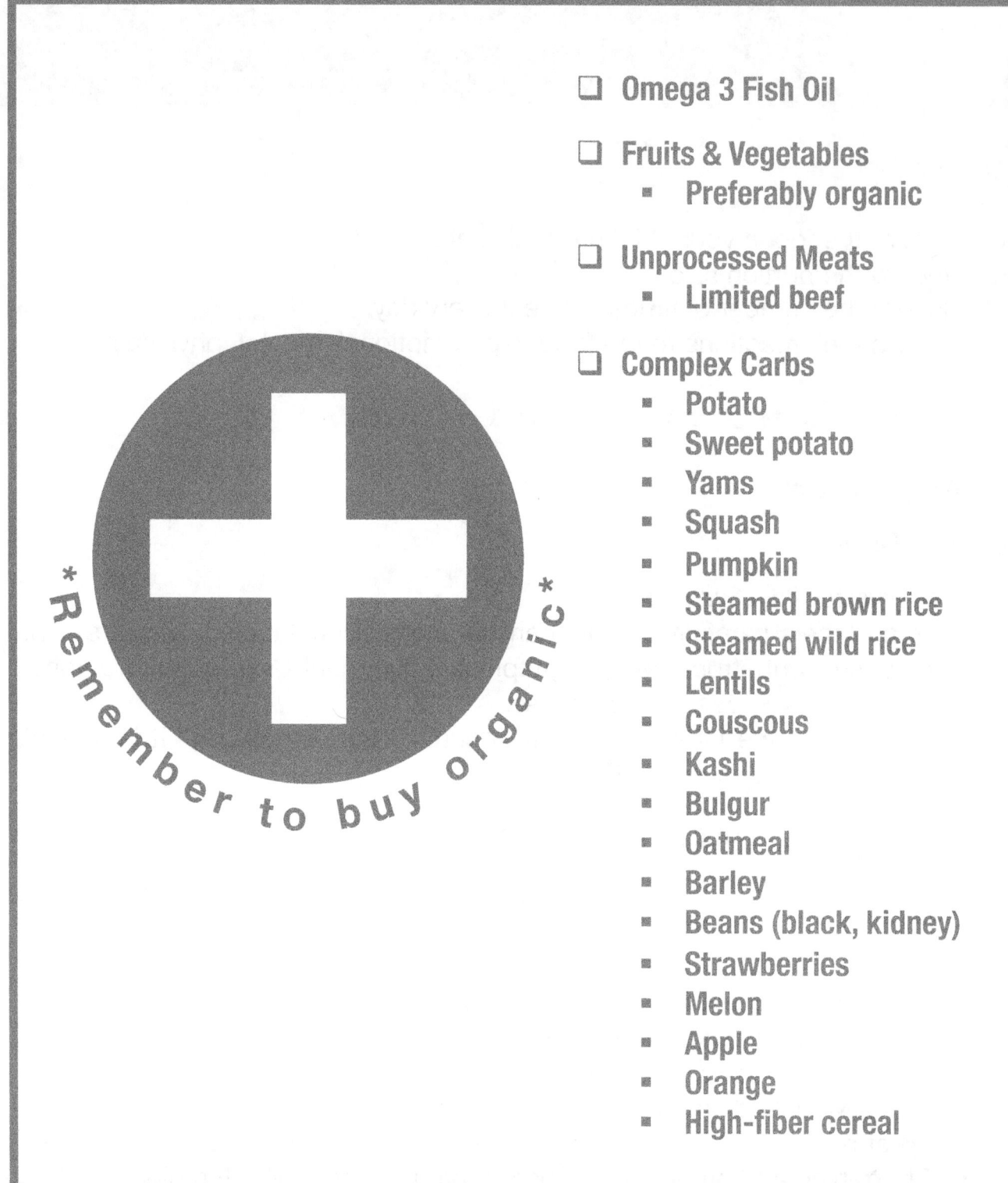

- ❏ Omega 3 Fish Oil
- ❏ Fruits & Vegetables
  - Preferably organic
- ❏ Unprocessed Meats
  - Limited beef
- ❏ Complex Carbs
  - Potato
  - Sweet potato
  - Yams
  - Squash
  - Pumpkin
  - Steamed brown rice
  - Steamed wild rice
  - Lentils
  - Couscous
  - Kashi
  - Bulgur
  - Oatmeal
  - Barley
  - Beans (black, kidney)
  - Strawberries
  - Melon
  - Apple
  - Orange
  - High-fiber cereal

Remember to buy organic

STEP №1: Assess their nutritional intake

notes

STEP №1: Assess their nutritional intake

STEP №2
Assess their level of physical activity

Consider What (if anything) The Child Is Doing Physically

- ❏ How often are they doing some form of exercise?
- ❏ For how long?
- ❏ Have they discovered something they enjoy doing?
  - They have a better chance of sticking with it if they enjoy doing the activity.
  - [For example, this is why I play soccer instead of running ☺].

Motor Develops The Brain!

REDUCE Television, computer time, smartphone, video games, and any other activity that involves a screen.

INCREASE Walking, bike riding, recreational sports, fitness programs, and any other opportunity for physical activity.

STEP №2: Assess their level of physical activity

notes

STEP No 3
Assess their social/emotional development

Real Self-Esteem Vs. Fake Self-Esteem

Building your child's identity is one of the single MOST important jobs of a parent!

When evaluating your child's situation...

- Keep in mind that the problems a child experiences can be either bigger or smaller than you think.
- A child with an imbalance in the brain can have SEVERAL deficits in Social/Emotional development.

 Ultimately, false self-esteem causes children to either lose respect for you or mistrust you.

Praising poor work as being good either...

- Invites distrust (i.e., you lied about their work being good).
- Provokes disrespect (i.e., you didn't realize their work was bad).

STEP №3: Assess their social/emotional development

notes

STEP №4
Assess your family time

Consider Your Family Time...Thoughtfully

As a family, do you have TIME to connect with your child(ren)?

Twenty years from now, what memories would you regret not having experienced with your child(ren)? You won't wish that...

- ...you'd spent more time counting the money in your bank account.
- ...you hugged your boss more.
- ...your house had more square footage.

BUT you might wish that you had used those precious moments of time with your family...DIFFERENTLY.

STEP №4: Assess your family time

Strategize Your Family Time Together

Connect with your kids away from distractions…electronic or otherwise.

① Create a weekly "electronic free evening" (no phones, no television, no computers, no screens!)

② Play games that reinforce your child's weaker hemisphere! (e.g., Right Brain = Charade's/Left Brain = Scrabble®).

③ In the car…create a music, phone, DVD, video game FREE zone and talk (be present with your child and find out what is going on in their world of school, friends, and interests).

④ Develop a family plan that invites input from every family member and the goals they are pursuing! (For all ages).

NOTE: Be aware of how much time your child(ren) spend doing homework and break it up into smaller chunks of time.

Reflect for a moment on your own childhood memories…which of those memories do you value the most? [I'm almost certain none of them involved doing homework ☺]. In all likelihood, the memories you treasure the most relate to what you did with your families.

However, if homework is unavoidable, at least break it up into smaller chunks. This will help to:

- *prevent* your child from feeling overwhelmed.
- *improve* comprehension.
- *build* a sense of personal accomplishment.
- …which, in turn, *strengthens* genuine self-esteem.

STEP №4: Assess your family time

notes

STEP Nº4: Assess your family time

TOOL №1
For your family life

It Is Important To Create Your Schedules As A Family.

No matter how scheduling has worked in the past [or not worked]...now you have some tools to begin developing a plan to reclaim your family!

① Assess nutrition.

② Assess physical activity.

③ Assess your child's emotional/social development.

④ Assess how you are spending time together as a family.

Carefully evaluating these four aspects of your family life will help you determine:

❏ Is this just "a kid being a kid"?

❏ Is there an imbalance that requires attention?

TOOL №1: For your family life

notes

TOOL №2
For your school life

Promote Balance And Connection In The Classroom

① Create motor breaks throughout the day.

② Create lessons and activities that pair motor with academics. (See **Appendix 4: The Activities Guide** on pp. 81-101).

③ Use color films to help the child focus when they read.

④ Play instrumental music while the child is completing independent tasks.

⑤ Teach concepts through singing.

⑥ Increase positive reinforcement and verbal affirmation (not false self-esteem building).

[Use this opportunity to experiment and find out what works best for your child.]

TOOL №2: For your school life

notes

TOOL Nº3
For your home life

Promote Balance And Connection In The Home

① Have the child sit on an exercise ball while completing homework.

② Use rewards and incentives for *effort*, not results.

③ Play high-pitched music (e.g., Michael Jackson; B-52's; R.E.M., etc.).

④ Use multiple sensory inputs at the same time.

⑤ Have the child play a musical instrument.

⑥ Have the child work on Word Searches.

⑦ Play Scrabble®, visual memory games, and crossword puzzles.

⑧ Have the child practice juggling.

NOTE: Your child's activities should be specific to their hemispheric weakness, so refer to **Appendix 4: The Activities Guide** on pages 81-101) before selecting their activities. But remember that no one knows your child better than you, so don't be afraid to experiment. ☺

TOOL №3: For your home life

notes

RECOMMENDED RESOURCES

DR. ROBERT MELILLO

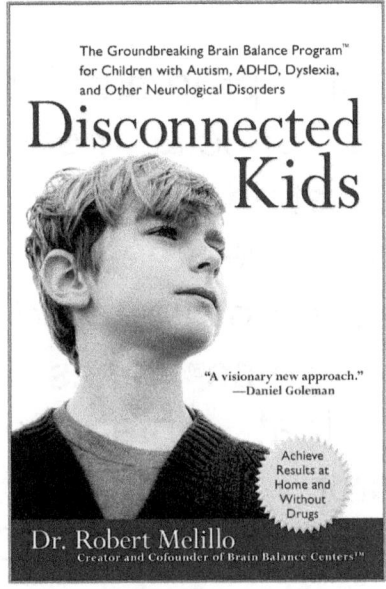

RECOMMENDED RESOURCES

DR. ROBERT MELILLO

Brain Balance®

Brain Balance® is a groundbreaking program that offers lasting improvement for special needs children. Instead of just cultivating a child's strengths or compensating for their weaknesses... they directly address the root causes of the child's developmental delays. Brain Balance® uses a uniquely holistic approach that integrates *individualized* (1) sensory motor training and stimulation, (2) cognitive activities, and (3) nutritional protocols.

On a personal note, during my tenure as Program Director for Brain Balance® of Austin, I was blessed to witness the *transformation* of children's lives and have the highest regard for their work. (BTW, I'm not a paid spokesman, just a huge fan).

www.brainbalancecenters.com

TABLE OF APPENDICES

APPENDIX 1: The Hemispheres Explained — 31

APPENDIX 2: The Primitive Reflexes — 43

APPENDIX 3: The Nutritional Guide — 61

APPENDIX 4: The Activities Guide — 73

APPENDIX 5: The Resource Guide — 103

No one lives any story but their own...

 **NOTE:** This content is for informational purposes only and is not intended as a medical diagnosis. You should consult a qualified professional for a full evaluation of your child's history and symptoms.

APPENDIX №1
THE HEMISPHERES EXPLAINED

Understanding what the Left and Right hemispheres of the brain do, and how they work together.

THE HEMISPHERES EXPLAINED

The Left Hemisphere sees the world in small pictures and ignores the big-picture to focus on the details. The left brain can be variously described as:

The Right Hemisphere sees the big-picture view of the world but misses the individual parts. In other words, it sees the forest but can't see the trees. The right brain can be variously described as:

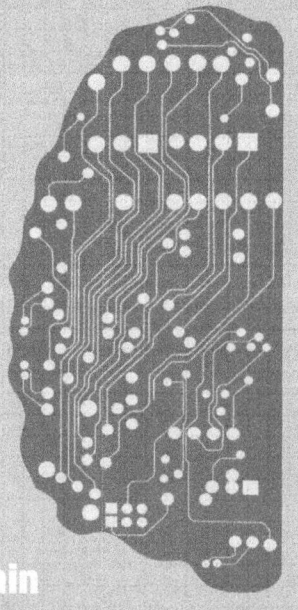

Left	Right
Small Muscle Brain	Big Muscle Brain
Literal Brain	Spatial Brain
Conscious Brain	Social Brain
Logical Brain	Subliminal Brain
Routine Brain	Curious Brain
Impulsive Brain	Safe Brain
Thinking Brain	Negative Brain
Curious Brain	Caution Brain
Positive Brain	Empathetic Brain
Processing Brain	Sensory Brain
Immune-Driving Brain	Immune-Inhibiting Brain

THE LEFT HEMISPHERE

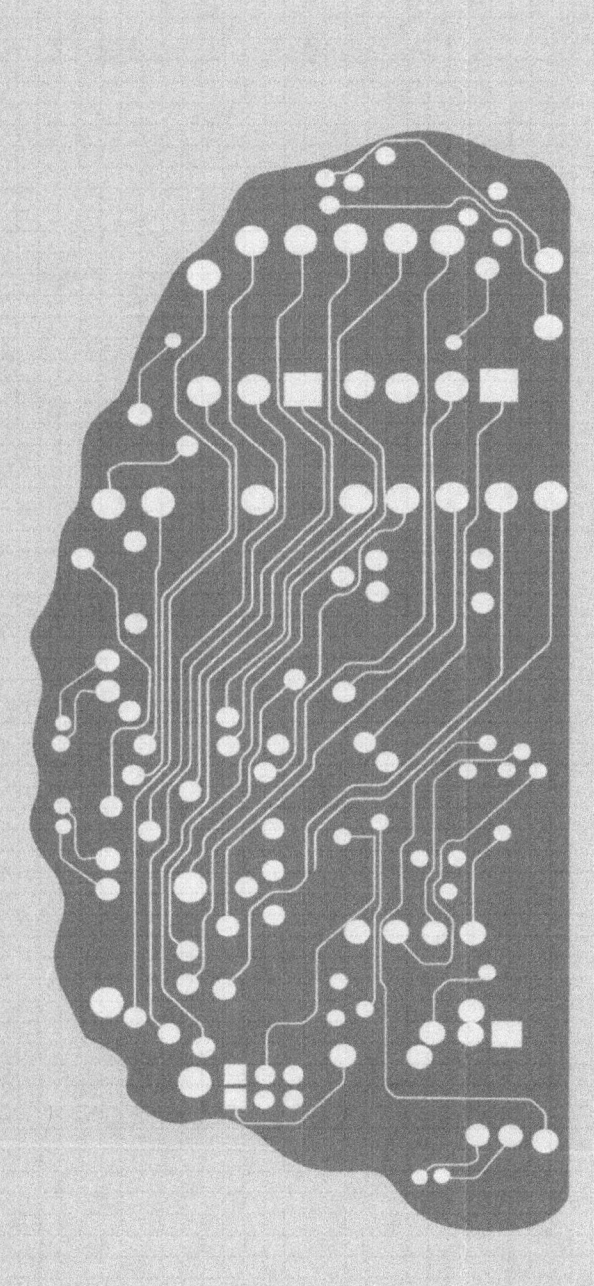

The Small Muscle Brain
...controls fine motor skills—everything done with the hands, fingers, feet, and toes (i.e., tying shoes and playing the piano). It also controls speech and the ability to translate sounds of letters and symbols into language.

The Literal Brain
...controls everything related to language—reading, writing, speaking and interpretation. It converts letters into syllables, syllables into words, and words into sentences. It reads individual words in a sentence and translates their meaning…letter by letter, and syllable by syllable.

The Conscious Brain
...is involved in every conscious move made by the body. It enables you to read a book, solve a math problem, or memorize a poem. It is also involved in creating conscious thoughts (i.e., talking to yourself).

THE LEFT HEMISPHERE

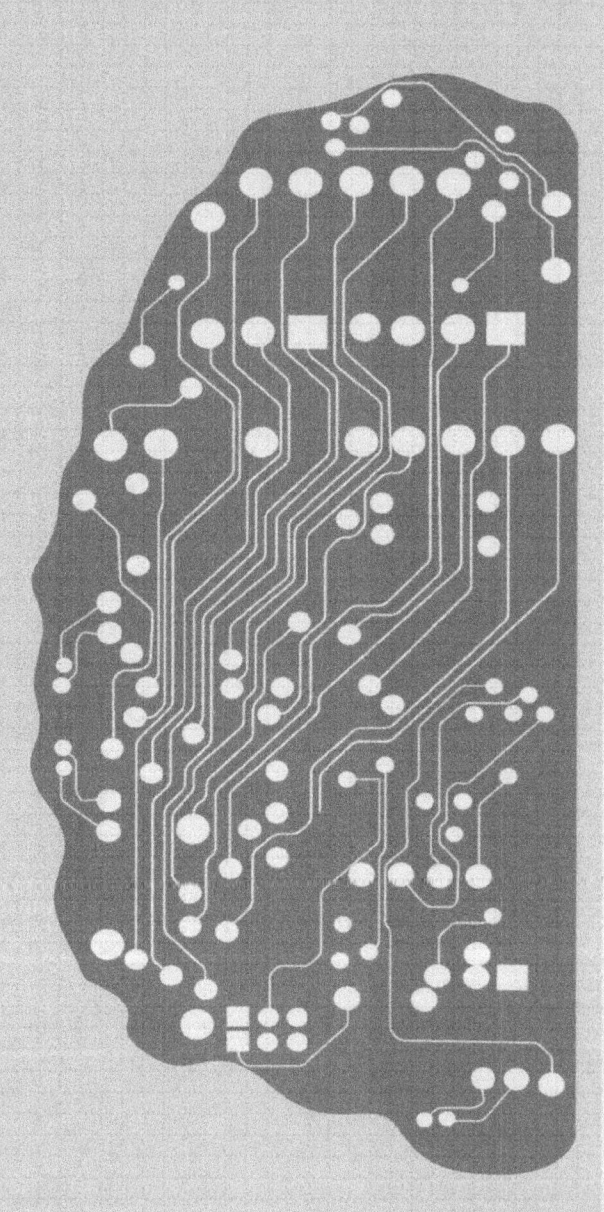

The Logical Brain
...is concerned with systemization; its thinking process is linear and logical as it examines things sequentially, one at a time, to determine patterns. It enjoys basic science, math, and other logical pursuits. Language develops because of pattern recognition skills (e.g., learning a new language or learning to play a musical instrument). Since computer/video games depend upon pattern recognition skills...this brain loves them.

The Routine Brain
...hates change and loves doing the same routine over and over. When you eat the same breakfast every day or stay at the same job even though you hate it...the left brain is in control of your thinking.

THE LEFT HEMISPHERE

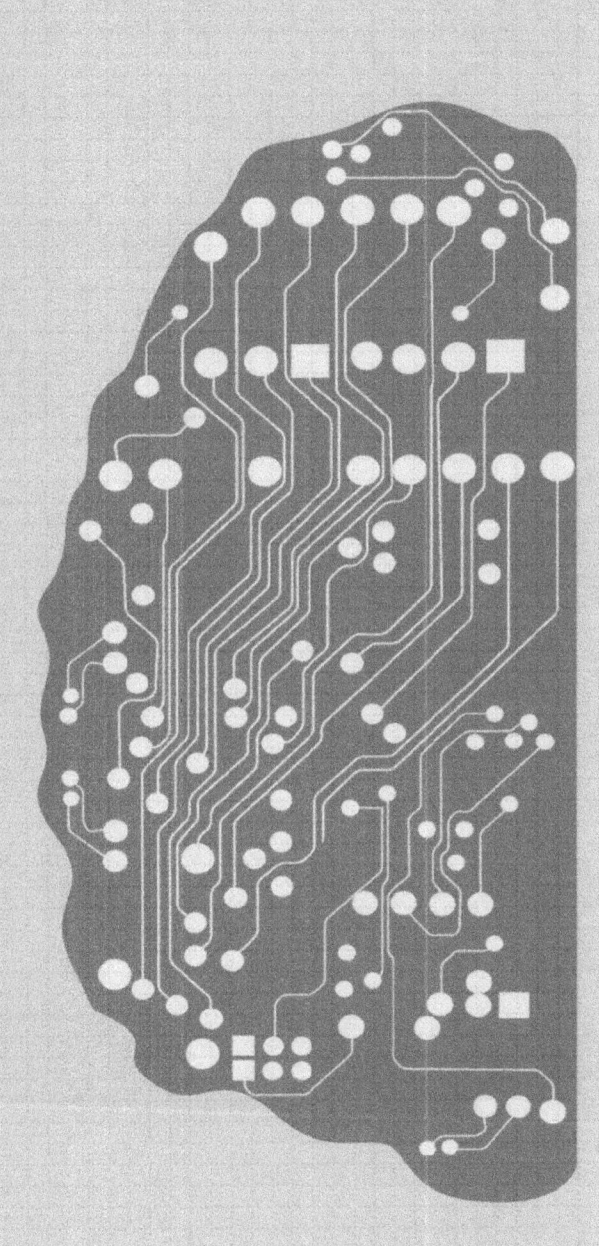

The Impulsive Brain
...loves taking risks (i.e., running a yellow light at an eight-way intersection during rush hour). Kids who don't "think-before-doing" are predominately using this brain.

The Thinking Brain
...if your child is "smart," this brain is probably stronger...which is primarily responsible for verbal intelligence. Traditional IQ tests measure left brain abilities more than right brain abilities.

The Curious Brain
...controls our behavioral approach (i.e., the fight part of our "fight-or-flight" instinct) by helping us determine whether to outsmart the lion in the jungle or run like crazy. It seeks to assess a situation, study all the details, figure it out, and remember it.

THE LEFT HEMISPHERE

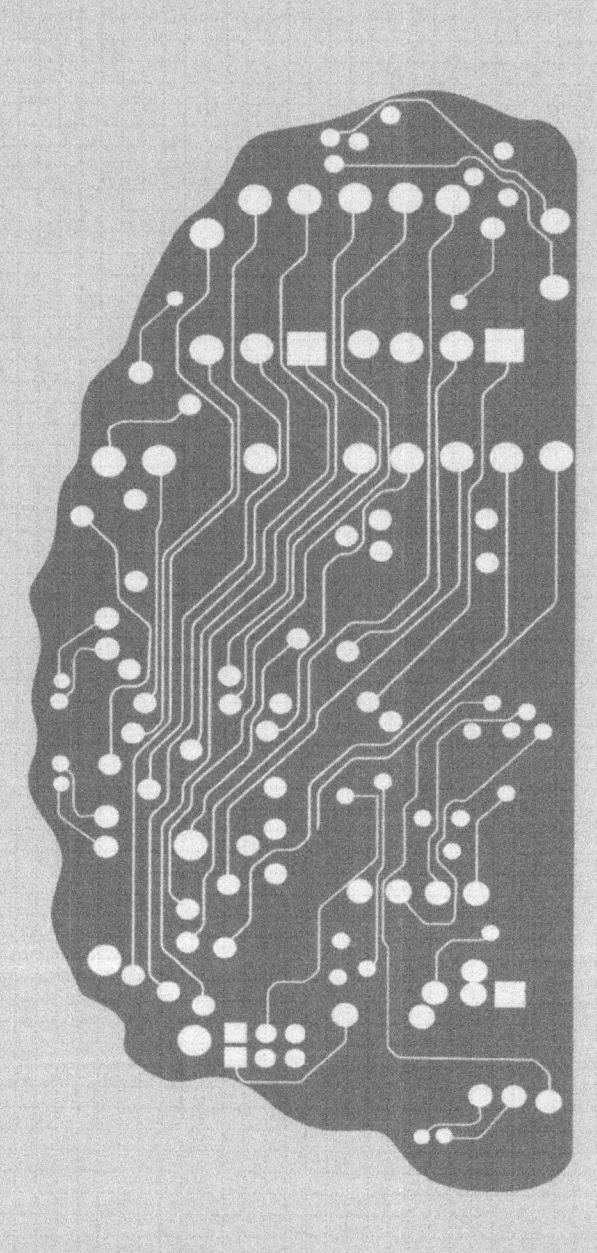

The Positive Brain
...is responsible for positive emotions and motivations (i.e., happiness, having fun, and personal energy).

The Processing Brain
...is responsible for processing high-frequency sounds and the details of visual images (which don't travel at the same speed). Perfect timing is essential for observing, listening, and understanding.

The Immune-Driving Brain
...mobilizes immune system antibodies to resist infection. It also stimulates the growth and development of lymphoid tissue that houses white blood cells and other chemicals. When a child is left-brain weak, they often get sick. But, when it's overactive, they can develop auto-immune problems (i.e., gastrointestinal problems, food allergies, etc.

THE RIGHT HEMISPHERE

The Big Muscle Brain
...controls movement of the major muscles, posture, and gait. It helps you climb the stairs or shake someone's hand.

The Spatial Brain
...allows you to feel yourself in space and controls balance and proprioception (i.e., the ability to know where your body is in relationship to gravity, to self, and to others).

The Social Brain
...is the nonverbal communicator and it reads body posture, facial expressions, and tone of voice to interpret what another person is thinking or feeling. Nonverbal communication lays the groundwork for the verbal communication that later develops on the left side…and is the foundation of socialization. Without nonverbal proficiency, social cues are missed, and verbal expression is nearly impossible.

THE RIGHT HEMISPHERE

The Subliminal Brain
...is nonverbal and learns subconsciously or subliminally (e.g., meeting a new person or learning a new face). This new image is then stored in the brain. This type of learning is called procedural or implicit memory.

The Curious Brain
...likes new situations or locations and hates repetition. Consequently, it becomes easily bored by routine.

The Safe Brain
...can sense right from wrong. It controls impulses and will prevent a child from acting out, especially when it is socially inappropriate.

THE RIGHT HEMISPHERE

The Negative Brain
...recognizes and identifies negative emotions, such as fear and anger.

The Caution Brain
...is governed by avoidance and a desire for self-protection (e.g., flee instead of fight). While the curious left brain wants to approach, the cautious right brain signals whether it is safe or dangerous. (e.g., slamming on your brakes at a yellow light).

The Empathetic Brain
...is concerned with emotional intelligence (EQ). Without learning to feel and read our own emotions, it is impossible to understand the emotions in other people. Our EQ enables us to know what another person is feeling/thinking because we know why we are feeling/thinking the same way. It is how we acquire empathy.

THE RIGHT HEMISPHERE

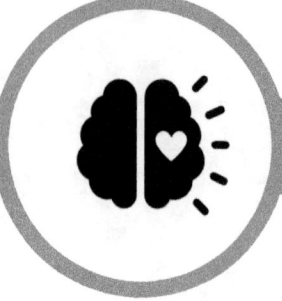

The Sensory Brain
...houses the sensory controls and therefore senses and feels the entire body. It regulates emotions that are internalized as a "churning gut," "pounding heart," and fast breathing. It is attuned to smell and taste, so if a smell is good, the right brain tells us the person or object is good; if the smell is bad, then it tells us the person or object should be avoided. It is also responsible for receiving information from the auditory system.

The Immune-Inhibiting Brain
...prevents the immune system from overreacting, so that it doesn't inadvertently activate its own protective antibodies and create autoimmune diseases.

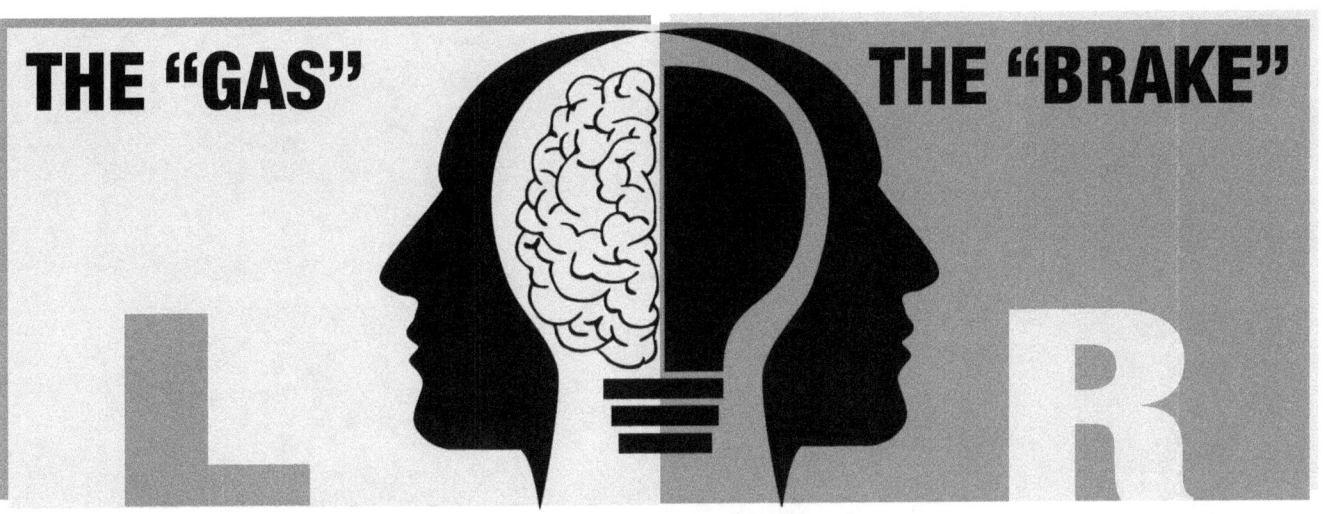

THE "GAS" (L)	THE "BRAKE" (R)
Small picture	Big picture
Serial processing	Parallel processing
Verbal communication	Nonverbal communication
Small (fine) muscle control	Large (gross) muscle control
IQ (intellectual intelligence)	EQ (emotional intelligence)
Reading words (phonemic awareness, decoding)	Reading comprehension (main idea, inference, pragmatics)
Math calculations (basic arithmetic operations)	Math reasoning (word problems, geometry)
Planning (theoretical)	Doing (practical)
Conscious actions; memory, learning	Unconscious actions; memory, learning
Explicit memory (declarative)	Implicit memory (procedural)
Positive emotions (approach)	Negative emotions (withdraw)
High-frequency sound	Low-frequency sound
Low-frequency vision	High-frequency vision
Light touch	Deep touch
Receiving auditory input	Interpreting auditory input
Linear and logical thinking	Abstract thinking
Curious, impulsive actions	Cautious, safe actions
Likes routine, sameness	Likes newness, novelty
Activates immunity; (+) antibody sensitivity	Suppresses immunity; (-) antibody sensitivity
Literal meaning	Metaphorical (alternative) meaning
Local spatial awareness	Global spatial awareness
Pleasant sense of taste and smell	Unpleasant sense of taste and smell
Social display (emotional motivation)	Social skills (emotional skills, empathy)
Intention	Attention
Motor	Sensory
Cause and effect	Present; "in the now"
Explaining	Describing
Practical, deliberate	Intuitive, gut feeling
Unconnected to body, digestion, and autonomic regulation	Connected to body, digestion, and autonomic regulation
Reduces stress, primarily on left side	Reduces whole body stress

APPENDIX №2
THE PRIMITIVE REFLEXES

Understanding the Primitive Reflexes: What to look for and how to identify if your child has retained them.

THE PRIMITIVE REFLEXES

Primitive Reflexes

The retention of primitive reflexes (which typically cease by 24 months of age) can be caused by a variety of factors, with the birth process being a key factor in the integration of these reflexes.

Consequently, retained primitive reflexes are usually triggered by...

- **a traumatic birth experience.**
- **birth by C-section.**
- **early falls or traumas.**
- **lack of tummy time.**
- **delayed or missed creeping or crawling.**
- **chronic ear infections.**
- **head trauma.**
- **vertebral subluxations.**

There are 70 known primitive reflexes, and eight of those reflexes are most commonly present in cases of Functional Disconnection Syndrome (FDS). Retention of these reflexes can inhibit a child's social, emotional, and cognitive development. Some retained reflex symptoms even overlap, which can compound the other symptoms.

In typical development, the **primitive reflexes** are replaced by the **postural reflexes** which control tiny equilibrating mechanisms that the brain needs for balance and coordination...after we have learned to sit, stand, and move from an upright position.

These reflexes enable us to live in harmony with gravity, to maintain a steady visual image even when we are moving (or the object is moving) and to edit nonessential stimuli which enables greater focus upon essential stimuli. They also play a major role in **proprioception**.

THE PRIMITIVE REFLEXES

What Is Proprioception?

Proprioception, or the body's ability to sense itself, can be quite complicated, especially in children with academic, social, or behavioral issues that have been labeled ADHD, Asperger's, and sensory processing disorders. Proprioceptive dysfunction has often been observed in such children, since they have trouble (1) knowing where their body is in space and (2) understanding social boundaries when playing and interacting with other children.

How Does It Work?

Proprioception is guided by receptors in the body (skin, muscles, joints) that connect with the brain through the nervous system so that even without sight, a person knows what his/her body is doing. Although vision plays a crucial role in the ability to sense one's body in space, it is not necessary in order for a person to understand body ownership. In fact, proprioception may already be present in newborns.

Proprioceptive Dysfunction

Many children with processing disorders report feeling scattered or disconnected...*which are likely related to a faulty sense of proprioception.* Children who are clumsy, uncoordinated, and sensory deficient are often experiencing proprioceptive dysfunction. The most common signs of this dysfunction are:

- **Sensory deficient:** The child pushes/writes too hard, plays rough, bangs or shakes feet while sitting, chews, bites, and likes tight clothes.

THE PRIMITIVE REFLEXES

- **Poor motor planning/control & body awareness:** The child has trouble going up and down stairs, frequently bumps into people and objects, and has difficulty riding a bike.

- **Poor postural control:** The child (1) slumps, is unable to stand on one foot, and needs to rest their head on a desk while working. (2) The child often self-regulates by engaging in behaviors that provide proprioceptive input (e.g., toe walking, crashing, running, or flapping).

One study reported that children with proprioceptive issues (1) experienced decreased motor planning and postural control which (2) resulted in disruptive behaviors that negatively affected their participation in daily tasks.

Regulating Proprioception

Tasks that involve heavy resistance and sensory input for the muscles and joints are *essential to regulating proprioception*. In fact, there is encouraging evidence suggesting that the sensorimotor cortex governing proprioception is not permanent and *can be changed through external exercises.*

Consequently, whenever proprioception is engaged, *there is hope that it can be improved* with the use of sensory integration therapies that specifically target proprioceptive stimulation.

For example, frog jumps, bear hugs, and climbing monkey bars are just a few of the activities that may help a child struggling with proprioceptive dysfunction.

PALMAR REFLEX | coordination/fine motor

The **Palmar Reflex** (birth to 5-6 months) is activated by the automatic flexing of an infant's fingers to grasp an object. For example, stimulating an infant's palm causes the hand to grasp and if you try to pull away, the grasp should get tighter. When this reflex is retained after six months, symptoms can include:

- ❑ Poor fine motor skills and manual dexterity.
- ❑ Inappropriate pencil grip and poor handwriting.
- ❑ Copying is easy but the task of spelling and writing words is difficult.
- ❑ The child often sticks their tongue out while writing.
- ❑ Intertwined speech and hand movement.
- ❑ Difficulty processing ideas on to paper.
- ❑ Poor posture when playing piano or working with the hands.
- ❑ Poor posture and/or back pain when working at a desk or computer.

MORO REFLEX | coordination/fine motor

The Moro Reflex (birth to 4 months) is activated to respond to unexpected changes within an infant's environment and acts as their "fight or flight" response.

For example, when an infant's head is unsupported, or they are startled by a loud noise, bright light, or sudden touch…the arms thrust outward and then curl in to embrace themselves. Typically, this reflex is replaced by the adult startle reflex. When this reflex is retained after four months, symptoms can include:

- ❑ Prone to sensory overload (i.e., over-sensitivity/over-reaction to sensory stimulus especially to bright lights).
- ❑ Tires easily under fluorescent lights.
- ❑ Difficulty focusing on more than one thing.
- ❑ Difficulty reading black print on white paper.
- ❑ Dislike of loud noises.
- ❑ Easily distracted.
- ❑ Poor impulse/emotional control.
- ❑ Prone to anxiety.
- ❑ Prone to aggression.
- ❑ Mood swings.
- ❑ Emotional/social immaturity.
- ❑ Motion sickness.
- ❑ Prone to allergies and weak immune systems.
- ❑ Poor balance/coordination (particularly playing ball games)…which leads to poor sequencing and memory skills.
- ❑ Withdrawn or timid.
- ❑ Dislike of change causes child to be clingy or shy.

ROOTING REFLEX | coordination/fine motor

The **Rooting Reflex** (birth to 3-4 months) is activated during the act of breastfeeding. A light touch on the infant's cheek, or stimulation to the edge of their mouth automatically causes the infant to turn their head toward the stimulation and open their mouth with an extended tongue to accept the nipple into their mouth.

A suppressed central nervous system may indicate developmental delays and when this reflex is retained after four months, symptoms can include:

- ❑ The child's tongue sits too forward in the mouth which can cause dribbling or problems with speech.
- ❑ Difficulty with solid foods.
- ❑ Prone to thumb sucking.
- ❑ Hypersensitivity around lips and mouth.
- ❑ Poor manual dexterity, especially when speaking.
- ❑ Poor articulation.
- ❑ Hormonal imbalances.
- ❑ Messy eater.

ASYMMETRICAL TONIC NECK REFLEX | coordination/fine motor

The **Asymmetrical Tonic Neck Reflex (ATNR)** (birth to 6 months) is activated when an infant is lying flat on their back with their head turned to one side causing the arm and leg on that side to extend or straighten, while the other arm and leg flex. The reflex should be fully present at birth and assists the infant's active participation in the birthing process.

This connection between touch and vision helps establish distance perception and hand-eye coordination. (i.e., ATNR locks vision on to anything that catches the attention). When this reflex is retained after six months, symptoms can include:

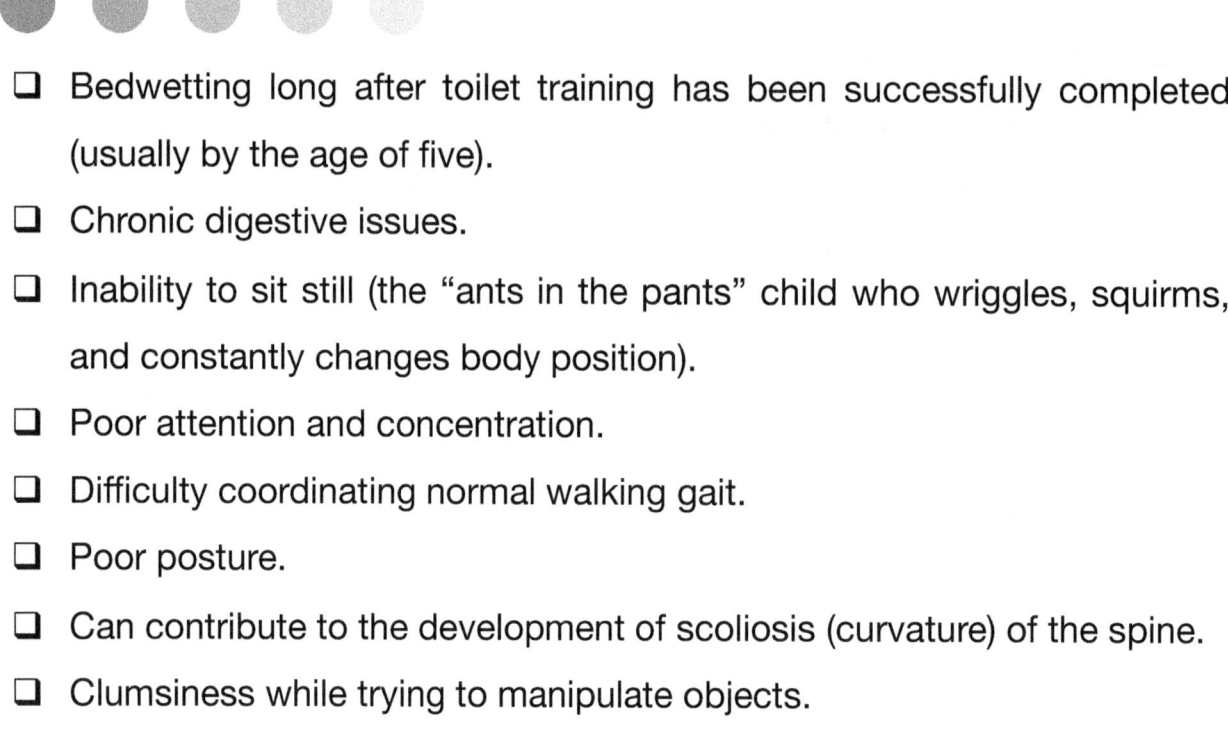

- ❏ Bedwetting long after toilet training has been successfully completed (usually by the age of five).
- ❏ Chronic digestive issues.
- ❏ Inability to sit still (the "ants in the pants" child who wriggles, squirms, and constantly changes body position).
- ❏ Poor attention and concentration.
- ❏ Difficulty coordinating normal walking gait.
- ❏ Poor posture.
- ❏ Can contribute to the development of scoliosis (curvature) of the spine.
- ❏ Clumsiness while trying to manipulate objects.
- ❏ Poor flexibility and mobility in physical activities or sports.

SPINAL GALANT REFLEX | postural/gross motor

The **Spinal Galant Reflex** (birth to 3-9 months) is activated when the skin along the side of an infant's back is stroked, causing them to move towards the side that was stroked (the stimulation of their lower back stimulates their hips). The reflex also plays an active role in the birth process, when hip movements assist the infant to work their way down the birth canal.

Simultaneous stimulation down both sides of the spine activates a related reflex, which causes urination (e.g., the stimulation of bed sheets can activate this reflex). When this reflex is retained after nine months, symptoms can include:

- ❏ Poor at sports; difficulty catching a ball.
- ❏ Poor hand-eye coordination.
- ❏ Poor distance perception.
- ❏ Easily distracted.
- ❏ Poor bilateral integration (integrated use of both sides of the body).
- ❏ Poor balance and clumsiness.
- ❏ Awkward pencil grip and poor handwriting.
- ❏ Unable to cross the vertical midline (e.g., a right-handed child may have difficulty writing on the left side of the page).
- ❏ Difficulty copying from a whiteboard.
- ❏ Poor visual tracking (necessary for reading and writing).
- ❏ Misses parts of a line when reading.
- ❏ Difficulty expressing ideas in written form.
- ❏ Difficulty establishing a dominant hand, eye, or ear.
- ❏ In adults: chronic shoulder and/or neck problems.
- ❏ Discrepancy between oral and written performance.

SYMMETRICAL TONIC NECK REFLEX | postural/gross motor

The **Symmetrical Tonic Neck Reflex (STNR)** (6-9 months to 9-11 months) is also known as the crawling reflex and presents briefly after birth and then reappears at 6 to 9 months. This reflex helps the body divide at the midline to assist in crawling…as the head is brought towards chest, the arms bend, and the legs extend. When this reflex is retained after eleven months, symptoms can include:

- ❏ Ability to crawl occurs later than normal.
- ❏ Poor hand-eye coordination.
- ❏ Poor muscle tone (especially of the spinal muscles).
- ❏ Poor posture (e.g., tends to slump sitting at a desk).
- ❏ An ape-like walking pattern.
- ❏ Focusing requires more effort, particularly on things that are close up.
- ❏ The eyes fatigue sooner than normal when focusing on near, then far objects.
- ❏ Copying from the whiteboard may be slow and tedious, causing them to miss large portions of classroom information.
- ❏ Poor organization and planning skills.
- ❏ Inability to sit still.
- ❏ Poor concentration
- ❏ Easily distracted.
- ❏ Difficulty playing ball games.
- ❏ Emotionally immature.
- ❏ Withdrawn or timid.
- ❏ Prone to anxiety.
- ❏ Prone to aggression.

LANDAU REFLEX | postural/gross motor

The **Landau Reflex** (4-5 months to 9-11 months) assists with postural development (but since it is not present at birth, it is not technically considered a primitive reflex). Lack of stimulation in the pre-frontal cortex causes attention, organization, and concentration problems.

It is activated when an infant (lying supine) lifts their head and raises their lower body with their upper body, causing the entire trunk to flex. When this reflex is retained after eleven months, symptoms can include:

- ❏ Poor short-term memory.
- ❏ Poor motor development.
- ❏ Low muscle tone.
- ❏ Poor posture.
- ❏ Poor balance.
- ❏ Tension in the back of legs; toe walker.
- ❏ Weak upper body.
- ❏ Difficulty swimming the breaststroke.
- ❏ Difficulty performing a somersault; knees buckle when the head tucks under.
- ❏ Awkward movement in lower half of the body.
- ❏ Stiff movements.
- ❏ Difficulty hopping, skipping, or jumping.

TONIC LABRYNTHINE REFLEX | postural/gross motor

The **Tonic Labyrinthine Reflex (TLR)** (in utero to 4 months) is activated when an infant is placed on their back and their head is tilted backwards. This movement causes their legs to straighten and stiffen, their toes to point, their hands to become fisted, and their elbows to bend.

The TLR forms the foundation of the vestibular system (sense of balance and position in space) and prepares the infant for rolling over, creeping, crawling, standing, and walking. When the reflex is present, an infant will experience a poor sense of balance when their eyes are closed. When this reflex is retained after 3.5 years, symptoms can include:

- ❏ A "floppy" child.
- ❏ Susceptible to motion sickness.
- ❏ Difficulty judging space, distance, depth, and speed.
- ❏ Poor self-orientation and spatial difficulties.
- ❏ Visual problems.
- ❏ Tendency to walk on toes.
- ❏ Poor balance.
- ❏ Difficulty coordinating movement.
- ❏ Sports performance below capability.
- ❏ Dislike of physical education and sports.
- ❏ Poor concentration.
- ❏ Fatigues easily while reading or when working or studying at a desk.
- ❏ Poor posture when working over a desk.
- ❏ Muscle tone (too weak/strong).
- ❏ Poor sense of rhythm/timing.

THE PRIMITIVE REFLEX EXERCISES

Repetition ▶ Frequency ▶ Consistency

The home exercises for the primitive reflexes work synergistically with the nutritional protocol to improve brain function, physical development, emotional maturity, and academic performance.

To see the *best improvement* in your child, be committed to completing the following exercises *exactly as described in the video*. Otherwise, your child will only experience *some improvement*. *The *proper form is critical.*

For your child to experience optimum improvement, complete the exercises *2x per day, 6 days per week*. However, if for any reason you are unable to complete both sets of exercises, just double the repetitions for that day.

In addition to following the nutritional protocol and completing the primitive reflex exercises, you can maximize your child's improvement by *limiting their screen time* (any exposure to TV, computer, phone, gaming, etc.) to 1 hour per day on weekdays and 2 hours per day on weekends.

Encourage your child to play outside, read, play board games, or do DIY projects instead. Remember…

- ❑ **The purpose of the exercises/repetitions/form is to fatigue the retained reflex.**
- ❑ **Frequency is more important than intensity.**
- ❑ **Movement must be slow and intentional (form is critical).**
- ❑ **The proper mind-set matters: stay motivated and be positive!**
- ❑ **Give it time.**

NOTE: The eye exercises from the **Exercise Journal** on page 59 can greatly enhance your protocol IF your child has already been evaluated by Brain Balance® or a vision therapist since they can determine if your child's situation involves eye tracking, comprehension, focus, etc.

PRIMITIVE REFLEX TEST

EXERCISE		NOTES	SCORES				
			0	1 25%	2 50%	3 75%	4 100%
ATNR	"Cat S/S"	Initial					
		5-week follow up					
MORO	"Trust Fall"	Initial					
		5-week follow up					
ROOTING	"Cat Whiskers"	Initial					
		5-week follow up					
PALMAR	"Hand Whiskers"	Initial					
		5-week follow up					
SPINAL GALANT	"Side Whiskers"	Initial					
		5-week follow up					
TLR	Standing "Head U/D"	Initial					
		5-week follow up					
	All fours "Head U/D"	Initial					
		5-week follow up					
STNR	"Zombie"	Initial					
		5-week follow up					
LANDAU	"Superman"	Initial					
		5-week follow up					

PRIMITIVE REFLEX TEST

EXERCISE		NOTES	SCORES				
			0	1 25%	2 50%	3 75%	4 100%
ATNR	"Cat S/S"	10-week follow up					
		15-week follow up					
MORO	"Trust Fall"	10-week follow up					
		15-week follow up					
ROOTING	"Cat Whiskers"	10-week follow up					
		15-week follow up					
PALMAR	"Hand Whiskers"	10-week follow up					
		15-week follow up					
SPINAL GALANT	"Side Whiskers"	10-week follow up					
		15-week follow up					
TLR	Standing "Head U/D"	10-week follow up					
		15-week follow up					
	All fours "Head U/D"	10-week follow up					
		15-week follow up					
STNR	"Zombie"	10-week follow up					
		15-week follow up					
LANDAU	"Superman"	10-week follow up					
		15-week follow up					

EXERCISE JOURNAL

	EXERCISE	MO	TU	WE	TH	FR	SA	SU
MORO	"Star Fish" (5-6x)	1	1	1	1	1	1	1
		2	2	2	2	2	2	2
ROOTING	Chew gum (1 hr.)	1	1	1	1	1	1	1
		2	2	2	2	2	2	2
	"Cat Whiskers" (10x R/L)	1	1	1	1	1	1	1
		2	2	2	2	2	2	2
PALMAR	"Ball Grasp" (25x R/L)	1	1	1	1	1	1	1
		2	2	2	2	2	2	2
	"Finger O's" (25x R/L)	1	1	1	1	1	1	1
		2	2	2	2	2	2	2
ATNR	"Lizard" (5-6x)	1	1	1	1	1	1	1
		2	2	2	2	2	2	2
	"Reverse Lizard" (5-6x)	1	1	1	1	1	1	1
		2	2	2	2	2	2	2
SPINAL GALANT	"Snow Angels" (5-6x)	1	1	1	1	1	1	1
		2	2	2	2	2	2	2
TLR	"Human Ball" (5-6x)	1	1	1	1	1	1	1
		2	2	2	2	2	2	2
STNR	"Cat" (5-6x)	1	1	1	1	1	1	1
		2	2	2	2	2	2	2
LANDAU	"Superman" (5-6x)	1	1	1	1	1	1	1
		2	2	2	2	2	2	2

EXERCISE JOURNAL

	EXERCISE	MO	TU	WE	TH	FR	SA	SU
CORE	PULL-UPS (up to 20)	1	1	1	1	1	1	1
	PUSH-UPS (up to 20)	2	2	2	2	2	2	2
	SIT-UPS (up to 50)	3	3	3	3	3	3	3
EYE	WIDE-EYE (1 minute)	1	1	1	1	1	1	1
		2	2	2	2	2	2	2
		3	3	3	3	3	3	3
	NEAR-FAR (1 minute)	1	1	1	1	1	1	1
		2	2	2	2	2	2	2
		3	3	3	3	3	3	3
	SLOW-EYE (1 minute)	1	1	1	1	1	1	1
		2	2	2	2	2	2	2
		3	3	3	3	3	3	3
	EYE-ALIGN "pencil" push-ups (1 minute)	1	1	1	1	1	1	1
		2	2	2	2	2	2	2
		3	3	3	3	3	3	3
TACTILE	BRUSHING (10x R Arm+Leg) (10x L Arm+Leg)	1	1	1	1	1	1	1
		2	2	2	2	2	2	2

NOTES

THE PRIMITIVE REFLEXES

APPENDIX №3
THE NUTRITIONAL GUIDE

Healthy and practical tips on how to address the nutritional challenges of developmental delays.

HOPE

THE NUTRITIONAL GUIDE

Food Allergies Vs. Food Sensitivities

Food allergy = an immediate reaction that signals the body to produce histamine. In extreme cases, an IgE reaction requires immediate medical attention.

Food sensitivity = a delayed IgG reaction that typically manifests in one to four days. Consequently, if you are not closely monitoring your child's food intake or working with a professional, it will be difficult to identify the connection between their consumption of a particular food and the inflammatory reaction that follows.

Food Sensitivities & Behavior

If your child has a food sensitivity, there is often a direct connection to behavioral and/or emotional challenges. For example, after drinking a glass of milk, a child's body begins producing cytokines and the resulting inflammation inside their brain manifests as emotional meltdowns, defiance, irritability, anxiety, depression, brain fog, et. al.

Of course, if your child's digestion has already been compromised (e.g., leaky gut syndrome) by food sensitivities, these reactions can be compounded. A leaky gut creates three basic problems: (1) it interferes with the absorption vitamins and minerals resulting in nutritional deficiencies, (2) it contributes to learning or behavioral struggles, and (3) it can trigger additional food sensitivities.

If you suspect that your child may be suffering from a food sensitivity, *I strongly urge you to seek professional advice.* Prior to your consultation with the nutritionist, it would be *highly beneficial* to log your child's food intake in the **7-Day Food Journal** on page 72.

THE NUTRITIONAL GUIDE

❑ Log all foods consumed (include both the quantity and the time of day).
❑ Log any resulting symptoms and/or behavior.

A clear pattern may emerge, but sometimes additional testing is required to confirm which foods are the true causes. Removing these foods from your child's diet can make a *huge* difference in their emotional, behavioral, mental, and physical state of being.

THE NUTRITIONAL GUIDE

BUY FOODS FREE FROM THE FOLLOWING INGREDIENTS

- ❏ Artificial sweeteners (e.g., acesulfame potassium, aspartame, cyclamate, saccharin, sucralose, Splenda®, Nutrasweet®, Equal®, et. al.).
- ❏ Artificial colorings/flavorings.
- ❏ Eggs.
- ❏ Gluten.
- ❏ High fructose corn syrup.
- ❏ Hydrogenated oils/trans-fats.
- ❏ Monosodium glutamate (MSG).
- ❏ Peanuts.
- ❏ Sodium nitrate & nitrites.
- ❏ Soy.

ALWAYS BUY THE FOLLOWING FOODS ORGANIC

- ❏ Apples
- ❏ Bell Peppers
- ❏ Blueberries
- ❏ Celery
- ❏ Cucumbers
- ❏ Grapes
- ❏ Lettuce
- ❏ Nectarines
- ❏ Peaches
- ❏ Potatoes
- ❏ Spinach
- ❏ Strawberries

THE NUTRITIONAL GUIDE

The so-called "dirty dozen" has been identified by a number of respected researchers and nutritional experts as the most common causes of food sensitivities/allergies.

Successful completion of the **90-Day Elimination Program** depends upon avoiding the twelve foods listed below for 90 days.

- ❏ ALL products containing wheat or gluten.
- ❏ ALL dairy and milk products (casein), including goat milk.
- ❏ ALL refined sugars.
- ❏ Apples (and other salicylates).
- ❏ Baker's & Brewer's yeast.
- ❏ Chocolate.
- ❏ Corn.
- ❏ Eggs.
- ❏ Legumes (beans, peas, peanuts, soy).
- ❏ Oranges (including all citrus fruits & juices).
- ❏ Soy.
- ❏ Tomatoes.

THE NUTRITIONAL GUIDE

One of the most challenging aspects to successfully completing the **90-Day Elimination Program** is figuring out what to buy. The guesswork can be overwhelming…not to mention time-consuming as you wander through the supermarket hoping that you're buying the right food items.

For your convenience, I've put together a non-exhaustive list of resources you can use to write out your shopping list. If you haven't already, I would also encourage you to purchase the all-in-one **90-Day Elimination Program Journal** which walks you step-by-step through the process and allows you to easily track your progress.

Every family has their preferences when it comes to food, so I would also encourage you to find a cookbook or some online recipes that you like. That way, you can just can swap out their ingredients for ingredients that are compliant with the **90-Day Elimination Program**.

NO STRESS SHOPPING!☺

SHOPPING LIST FOR DAIRY

CHEESE

- ❏ Daiya® (www.daiyafoods.com)
  - cream cheese
  - GF DF pizzas
  - shredded cheese
  - wedge cheese

YOGURT

- ❏ So Delicious® (www.sodeliciousdairyfree.com)
  - coconut yogurt (plain for low-sugar content)

MILK

- ❏ Blue Diamond®
- ❏ Pacific®
- ❏ Rice Dream®
- ❏ So Delicious®
- ❏ Tempt®
  - All of the above brands also offer almond, coconut, rice, oat, hazelnut, hemp.

ICE CREAM

- ❏ NadaMoo® (www.nadamoo.com)
- ❏ So Delicious®

BUTTER

- ❏ Earth Balance® (soy-free)
- ❏ Ghee (clarified butter)

SHOPPING LIST FOR GRAINS

BARS & COOKIES

Bars
- ❑ Enjoy Life® (Mixed Berry, Sunbutter Crunch, Caramel Apple, Cocoa Loco)

Cookies
- ❑ Enjoy Life® (all varieties)

BREAD & TORTILLAS

Bread
- ❑ Enjoy Life® (gluten-free/egg-free)
- ❑ Food for Life® (brown rice)

Tortillas
- ❑ El Milagro® (corn)
- ❑ Food for Life® (brown rice)

Pizza Crust
- ❑ Bob's Red Mill® (gluten-free pizza crust mix)

CRACKERS

Rice Crackers
- ❑ Blue Diamond® Artisan Nut Thins
- ❑ Crunchmaster® (www.crunchmaster.com)

SHOPPING LIST FOR MEAT

NITRITE-FREE PREPARED MEATS

Sausages & Hot Dogs
- ❑ Applegate® (www.applegate.com)
- ❑ Coleman Han's® (pre-cooked chicken sausages)
- ❑ Diestal® (turkey patties) (www.diestalturkey.com)
- ❑ Pederson's® (pre-cooked sausages)
- ❑ Wellshire® (www.wellshirefarms.com)

Bacon
- ❑ Central Market® (only certain varieties, read label)
- ❑ Hormel® (only certain varieties, read label)
- ❑ Pederson's® (www.pedersonsfarms.com)

Lunch Meat
- ❑ Applegate® (turkey, chicken, pepperoni)
- ❑ Central Market® (only certain varieties, read label)
- ❑ Diestal®
- ❑ Hormel® (only certain varieties, read label)

Jerky
- ❑ Steve's Paleo Jerky® (gluten-free, soy-free) (www.myjerkyshop.com)

SHOPPING LIST FOR CONDIMENTS, EGGS, & NUTS

CONDIMENTS

❑ Nomato® (tomato-free ketchup, BBQ, pizza, pasta sauce) (www.nomato.com)

EGGS

Mayonnaise
❑ Earth Balance Mindful Mayo® (www.earthbalancenatural.com)
❑ Soy-Free Vegenaise® (www.followyourheart.com)

Leavening & Binding Alternatives
❑ Chia/Flax egg (1tb. ground chia/flax + 3tbs. water = 1 egg)
❑ Ener-G Egg Replacer® (baked goods)

NUTS

Nut butters (cashew, almond, sunflower)
❑ Justin's® (individual packets) (www.justins.com)
❑ Sun Butter® (www.sunbutter.com)

SHOPPING LIST FOR SNACKS

READ THE LABELS AND BUY ORGANIC

SNACKS & LUNCHES

- ❑ Apples* w/cashew butter
- ❑ Brown rice noodles w/tomato sauce
- ❑ Carrots/rice crackers w/hummus*
- ❑ Celery w/almond butter
- ❑ Chicken (grilled strips) w/dairy-free ranch
- ❑ Chocolate* (organic, dark)
- ❑ Cucumber's w/hummus*
- ❑ Dried fruit & nuts*
- ❑ Frozen grapes, pineapple, mango, banana (blended into "ice cream")
- ❑ Garbanzo beans* (roasted)
- ❑ Hot Dog (nitrate-free)
- ❑ Kale chips
- ❑ Lunch meat roll-up (nitrate-free) w/pesto
- ❑ Olives
- ❑ Pepperoni (nitrate-free) w/rice crackers
- ❑ Pickles (pickled vegetables)
- ❑ Potatoes (roasted) w/ketchup or aioli
- ❑ Pretzels (gluten-free)
- ❑ Rice cakes w/nut butter, hummus*, pesto
- ❑ Smoothie*

NOTE: When doing the 90-Day Elimination Program, items marked with an * should be replaced with an appropriate substitute.

7-DAY FOOD JOURNAL

DAY NO. ___	Mo Tu We Th Fr Sa Su (CIRCLE THE DAY YOU ARE RECORDING)
BREAKFAST	
	❑ Negative ❑ Same ❑ Positive
LUNCH	
	❑ Negative ❑ Same ❑ Positive
DINNER	
	❑ Negative ❑ Same ❑ Positive
SNACK	
	❑ Negative ❑ Same ❑ Positive
PHYSICAL OR COGNITIVE RESPONSE(S)	
BEHAVIORAL RESPONSE(S)	
ADDITIONAL COMMENTS	

APPENDIX №4

THE ACTIVITIES GUIDE

"Do's" and "Don'ts" based upon on your child's left/right hemispheric strengths and weaknesses.

UNDERSTANDING THE IMBALANCE

LEFT BRAIN WEAKNESS

- ❏ Poor math skills
- ❏ Poor verbal skills
- ❏ Poor spelling skills
- ❏ Poor reading skills
- ❏ Poor letter recognition
- ❏ Poor memory for details
- ❏ Fine motor problems
- ❏ Poor auditory processing
- ❏ Misses small details
- ❏ Weak immune response
- ❏ Poor self-esteem
- ❏ Poor motivation
- ❏ Task avoidance

RIGHT BRAIN WEAKNESS

- ❏ Awkward/clumsy
- ❏ Hyperactive/anxious
- ❏ Poor non-verbal skills
- ❏ Impulsive/lacks focus
- ❏ Poor emotional control
- ❏ Poor reading comprehension
- ❏ Obsessive/repetitive behaviors
- ❏ Immature social behavior
- ❏ Allergies/auto-immunities
- ❏ Lacks interest in sports
- ❏ Misses the "big picture"
- ❏ Poor eye contact
- ❏ "Space invader"

UNDERSTANDING THE IMBALANCE

LEFT BRAIN WEAKNESS
is most often "diagnosed" as…

- Language Delays
- Auditory Processing Disorders
- Dyslexia
- Learning Disabilities (Academic)

RIGHT BRAIN WEAKNESS
is most often "diagnosed" as…

- ADHD/ADD
- Asperger's Syndrome
- Autism
- Non-verbal Learning Disabilities
- Tourette's Syndrome
- Obsessive/Compulsive Disorders
- Bi-Polar Disorder

UNDERSTANDING THE IMBALANCE

When a child is only able to use one hemisphere of their brain, their ability to function at their best is limited. That's why it's so imperative for their brain to develop the ability to use both hemispheres simultaneously in order thrive emotionally, socially, and academically.

The left and right hemispheres of the brain control very different functions…usually the opposite functions. Therefore, *stimulating only the weaker hemisphere* will increase your child's functions and brain connectivity at a faster rate.

Although all children are unique and don't all share the same symptoms, as a *general rule*, your child will struggle more with skills connected to the *weaker hemisphere*.

In fact, they are likely already avoiding many of the skills controlled by the weaker hemisphere simply because those areas are underdeveloped, and he or she doesn't quite have the necessary abilities.

Unsurprisingly, it can be difficult to "inspire" the child to engage in the activities that stimulate their weaker side. So…just start at whatever level they are, and gradually work up to where they need to be. It's like training for a marathon. You don't suddenly wake up one day and run 26 miles. Instead, you train consistently to build your endurance over time.

When choosing activities for your child to do, it's important to consider the level of their abilities. For example, if they lack core strength, balance, or appropriate eye control, riding a bike would not be a good idea.

- ❑ Until those basic abilities are properly developed (and they will be), having them attempt to ride a bike will only result in frustration for both you and your child.

- ❑ Depending on their level of ability, begin with the simplest steps and then help them along as necessary.
    - Ex.: Perhaps they need to practice core exercises until they have the appropriate skill to ride a bike. Or, if their starting point is more advanced, they could begin with a tricycle, or a scooter.

UNDERSTANDING THE IMBALANCE

Activities that engage the left and right hemispheres are designed to develop two types of skills.

In nearly every instance in which a child has been assessed with a developmental delay (in at least one area)…they will struggle with learning or behavioral issues. Without exception, these children have inadequately developed motor and sensory systems and often demonstrate a lack of coordination, clumsiness, or an awkward gait.

Motor Skills Involve Several Different Activities

❏ Muscle tone, strength, and coordination.
❏ Rhythm and timing.
❏ Bilateral coordination [using both sides of the body together to perform a task].
❏ Gross and fine-motor skills.
❏ Primitive and postural reflexes.
❏ Eye-muscle development and coordination.
❏ Vestibular coordination [balance and posture].

UNDERSTANDING THE IMBALANCE

The causes of underdeveloped motor skills also apply to sensory delays in hearing, vision, smell, taste, touch, and balance. These sensory functions do not operate in isolation and are interdependently connected to one another. Together, these functions rely upon an appropriate level of stimulation and development in order to improve.

Sensory Skills Involve Several Different Activities

- Hearing.
- Vision.
- Smell.
- Taste.
- Touch.
- Vestibular [inner ear].
- Proprioception [ability to sense one's body in space].
- Balance and spatial perception.

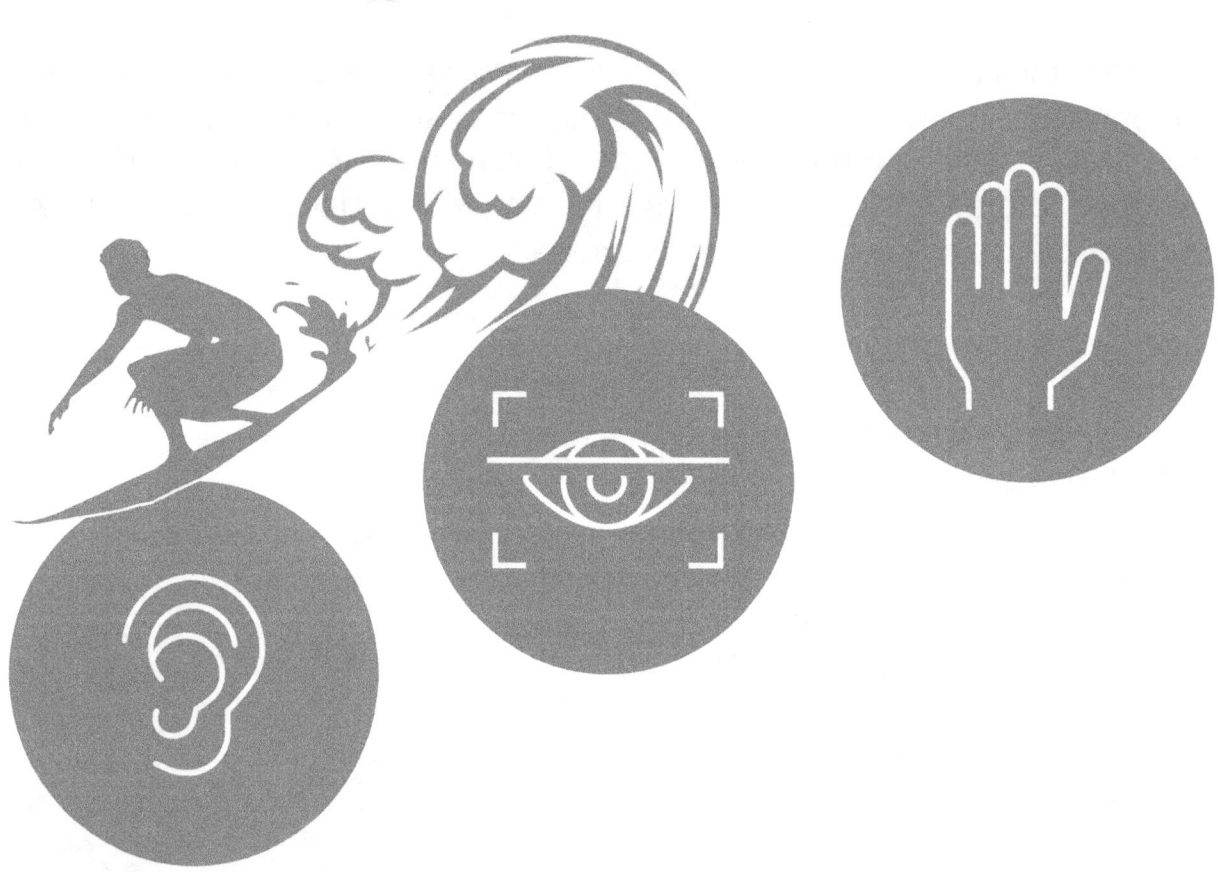

UNDERSTANDING THE IMBALANCE

The Seven Key Factors That Influence A Child's Self-Motivation

1. **Sense of control.** When a child is given a say in the decisions and choices that shape their world (age-appropriate, of course), they become more self-motivated. The scientific term for this is "internal locus of control", which studies have found to be correlated with higher motivation.

2. **Self-efficacy.** Encouraging a "growth mindset" increases a child's confidence in growing their capabilities because when they *believe in their ability* to accomplish things, their self-motivation improves.

3. **Parent-child relationship.** Nurturing supportive bonds with a child elevates their motivation, especially since they are like sponges, absorbing the attitudes *we model for them*.

4. **Peer influence.** The motivational impact of peers on a child is twofold: (1) through social pressure and (2) through fostering a sense of belonging within a group. Therefore, encouraging *positive* peer interactions significantly boosts a child's drive and enthusiasm.

5. **Goal orientation.** The greater a child's interest in achieving a specific mastery goal, the greater their motivation. Thus, in order to successfully help them set goals, it should be anchored in a genuine interest or desire.

6. **Physical and emotional well-being.** A child's motivation is also connected to their health. Consequently, persistent illness or emotional distress diverts their focus and energy, which negatively impacts their motivation.

7. **Embrace a growth mindset.** This a belief that abilities can be developed through perseverance, dedication, and hard work. It is the understanding that talents and skills are not fixed, but rather improve through effort. This mindset encourages children to embrace challenges, persist through setbacks, and view excellence of effort as the path to mastery and competence. This approach is arguably the cornerstone of encouraging the development of self-motivated children.

UNDERSTANDING THE IMBALANCE

LEFT And RIGHT Brain Activities

The following list of activities is divided into two categories:

- *Left Brain Weak* and *Right Brain Weak.*

These activities have been further divided into two subcategories:

- *Large Motor* and *Small Motor.*

Although the activities for *Left Brain Weak* and *Right Brain Weak* are nearly identical, there are small but *very important differences* concerning HOW to perform the activities.

IF YOUR CHILD IS LEFT BRAIN WEAK

- ❑ **Encourage anything that involves a large degree of detail**
  - Ex.: Use a detailed picture to build with Legos®.
  - Narrate stories but focus on the details rather than the moral/theme. Ask your child character names, the number of people he/she met, etc.
  - Work through mathematical story problems.

- ❑ **Encourage repetition**
  - Play memory games or practice flash cards.

- ❑ **Encourage activities involving letters**
  - Do crossword puzzles, word searches or other word games.
  - Read fact-based books or educational books.

- ❑ **Encourage activities involving numbers**
  - Play games involving numbers like Sudoku®, math games, counting, card games (e.g., Uno®).
  - Encourage your child to count their exercises aloud.

- ❑ **Encourage planning and scheduling**
  - Help your child plan out their schedule for the day, week, and month.

- ❑ **Encourage memory games or practicing memorization**
  - Play memory match games, memorize facts, details, books, or basic math facts.

- ❑ **Encourage linear or logical thinking or activities**
  - Ex.: Analytical games…chess, checkers, Risk®, or Stratego®.

- ❑ **Encourage light touch**
  - Ex.: soft tickling or touch only on the RIGHT side of the body.

IF YOUR CHILD IS LEFT BRAIN WEAK

❑ **Encourage listening to high frequency sounds**

- Ex.: Listen to high pitched sounds and instruments such as the violin, flute, etc.
- Listen to very fast, high-pitched music or rock and roll…and especially music with lots of words.

IF YOUR CHILD IS LEFT BRAIN WEAK

ACTIVITY	LARGE MOTOR DESCRIPTION
Badminton	Improves hand-eye coordination. Make sure your child remains active during the game and keep track of the score!
Baseball	Improves hand-eye coordination. Make everyone run the bases in between each batter and keep track of the score!
Basketball	Play full court to increase running and movement. If possible, lower the basket for easier shooting. Make everyone do laps around the court after each basket and keep track of the score!
Bikes/Scooters	Start out slow (with training wheels if needed) and see if your child can remember the way back home. Gradually build up to going faster, doing hills, etc.
Bean Bag Toss	Start close and then move farther back each time. You can also toss it back and forth to each other as well.
Bounce House	Great for jumping, bouncing, and the cross-crawl motion of climbing up the ladders, etc. Just keep them moving!
Bowling	Make sure the ball isn't too heavy for your child. Demonstrate the proper form and where to aim. Bowl with bumpers to help them be more successful and keep track of the score!
Camping	Exposes your child to new environments and experiences. Go on hikes and sing campfire songs. Be sure to take special notice of trees, animals, and the beautiful surroundings.
Croquet	Improves hand-eye coordination. Make sure your child remains active during the game and keep track of the score!
Dancing	Put on the music and just have a good time. Try to encourage big muscle movements. Teach your child steps involving rhythm and timing and help them (if able) to memorize a routine.
Dodgeball	Use a larger ball to make it easier to catch. Instruct everyone not to throw too hard or at the face. Make sure they stay active during the game and encourage them to develop strategies to win.
Fishing	Instruct your child on proper techniques and while waiting for the fish to bite, tell each other detailed stories (i.e., character names, places they went, order of events, etc.).

IF YOUR CHILD IS LEFT BRAIN WEAK

ACTIVITY	LARGE MOTOR DESCRIPTION
Flag Football	Make sure the game isn't overly rough. If your child has difficulty catching the ball, hand it off instead and get them running! Have fun but keep track of the score!
Frisbee	Keep your child moving and running to make the catch. But, if catching is too difficult, just throw the frisbee towards them and have them try to dodge it instead. Encourage your child to count how long it takes for the frisbee to get to them.
Golf	Mini- or regular golf, go to the driving range, or even just hit balls in a field. If you go to a course, don't use a cart and teach your child to keep score.
Gymnastics	Improves balance and core strength! Your child can do this at home, or you can enroll them in classes!
Hiking/Climbing	Indoor/outdoor hikes that accommodate your child's endurance level before consistently increasing the intensity over time.
Hockey	Use rollerblades if possible and play with taped brooms and balls in the street and remember to keep score.
Hokey Pokey	Use exaggerated movements and complete the steps in the same way to see if your child can remember the order.
Hoola Hoop®	Encourage your child to spin it around their arm, leg, waist, or neck…or just have them roll it on the ground without letting the hoop fall over.
Hopscotch	Indoor/outdoor hopscotch with tape/chalk as appropriate but encourage your child to say the numbers aloud as they step on them.
Horseback Riding	Improves core strength and balance.
Hot Potato	Stand in a circle and pass around an object. Play the appropriate music and when it stops, whoever is holding the object is out.
Ice Blocking	Buy a large block of ice, fold up a towel and place it on the block. Find a grassy large hill and encourage your child to sit on the block to slide down the hill. Make sure they push their own ice block back up the hill each time.

IF YOUR CHILD IS LEFT BRAIN WEAK

ACTIVITY	LARGE MOTOR DESCRIPTION
Ice Skating	Hold on tightly to your child if they have difficulty with balance and just be patient until their balance improves. ☺
Jump Rope	Set the rope on the ground and have the person at each end make it wiggle like a snake while your child jumps over it. Work up to having them jump rope on their own by having two people turn the rope as they jump…or tie one side to a doorknob while you hold the other. Have your child jump to the beat of a song or math problem. Ex.: 2 + 3 = 5, so jump 5 times.
Karate	Builds discipline, self-esteem, physical movement, and coordination. Make sure your child is able to follow directions and sit still before attempting this since most dojos don't allow kids to run around.
Kayaking	Be careful (wear a life jacket) and make sure your child helps you paddle.
Kickball	If your child has difficulty kicking the ball while it's rolling, place it in front of them instead. Make sure they run the bases as fast at they can and keep track of the score!
Laser Tag	Encourage your child to remain active during the game and have them to develop a strategy to win.
Obstacle Course	Indoor/outdoor using pillows, blankets, chairs, tables, etc. Time your child to see how fast they complete each round.
Paint Ball	Be careful! ☺
Parks	Encourage your child to give you directions to the park they want to play at and keep them active while they are there.
Playing Catch	Start with a bigger ball and stand closer together until your child becomes comfortable being farther away.
Potato Sack Race	Use pillowcases for the race and encourage your child to run hard enough to get good exercise.

IF YOUR CHILD IS LEFT BRAIN WEAK

ACTIVITY	LARGE MOTOR DESCRIPTION
Red Rover	Keep it fun! If your child becomes frustrated from being unable to break through, make sure someone lets them through. Increase the activity level by having them run laps between each turn.
Relay Races	Use activities that combine fine motor skills with racing (e.g., carrying an egg on a spoon, etc.).
Ring Around the Rosies	Encourage your child to spin counter-clockwise.
Ring Toss	If your child struggles with this activity, encourage them to start closer so they can be successful. Make sure they keep score.
Running/ Jogging	Encourage your child to practice math facts or spelling words while running.
Skiing/ Snow-boarding	Improves core strength and balance.
Slip n' Slide®	Use the Slip n' Slide® (or a long role of painters' plastic) in your backyard or nearby grassy hill.
Soccer	Improves coordination. Teach your child the rules of the game and how to keep score.
Sock Snowball Fights	Encourage your child to develop a strategy to win. Use rolled up socks for "snowballs" and then run, jump, duck, and dodge!
Stair Climbing	Encourage your child to run up and down stairs. Make it a relay race by placing something at the top of the stairs to grab and pass on to the next runner. If you don't have stairs, just have your child run in place, or march around the house while singing songs.
Swimming	Encourage your child to work on their swimming strokes instead of just splashing around.

IF YOUR CHILD IS LEFT BRAIN WEAK

ACTIVITY	LARGE MOTOR DESCRIPTION
T-ball	Improves hand-eye coordination and is great for children who aren't ready for baseball yet. Make sure your child runs the bases as fast as they can!
Tennis	Improves motor movements, hand-eye coordination, rhythm, and timing, BUT make sure your child is ready for this because it can be challenging to simultaneously move and hit the ball. Start with having them hit the ball against the wall or bounce it on the racquet before progressing to playing the game.
Trampoline	Encourage your child to try different simple tricks or even take them to trampoline arenas and bounce houses.
Volleyball	Improves hand-eye coordination.
Walking	Start with short walks and gradually increase the distance each time until your child's endurance improves.
Water Fights	Water balloon volleyball is really fun! Have two kids hold each end of a towel and place a water balloon on it. Toss it over the net to other players or toss it up and down while trying to catch it on the towel. Have them around the yard and throw water balloons or wet sponges at each other.
Waterskiing Wakeboarding Kneeboarding Tubing	Improves balance and is a great workout (and lots of fun)!
Weightlifting	Start with light weights and increase the amount each time until your child's strength improves.
Wrestling	Basic wrestling and roughhousing is great fun and exercise but be careful! ☺
Yoga	Learn some basic children's yoga (check YouTube®) and then practice it consistently with your child. Make sure they perform their deep breathing exercises.

IF YOUR CHILD IS LEFT BRAIN WEAK

ACTIVITY	SMALL MOTOR DESCRIPTION
Clay/Dough	Gluten-free only (Play-Dough® is not). If your child can follow step-by-step instructions, then make something and see if they can copy what you made.
Coloring	Focus on staying inside the lines.
Crochet	Excellent for developing fine motor skills. It also encourages synchronization because your child is using both their hands simultaneously.
Cross Stitch	Excellent for developing fine motor skills.
Finger Painting	Excellent for developing fine motor skills and tactile skills. Encourage your child to paint on big posters, old T-shirts, or even with their toes!
Lacing Cards	Make sure your child uses their RIGHT hand.
Moonsand/Moondough	Excellent for developing fine motor skills and tactile skills
Operation®	Assess your child's level of ability and if necessary...turn off the buzzer to prevent frustration...allow them to use tweezers to grab the objects...time them to see how fast they can collect all the objects (speed helps develop fine motor).
Painting	Excellent for developing fine motor skills. Encourage your child to paint something as simple as watercolors or water books...or more advanced like enrolling them in art classes, etc.
Perfection®	Excellent for developing fine motor skills and speed. Start by having your child only use their RIGHT hand during the game. To improve synchronization, place a pile of disks on either side of them and make sure they use both hands simultaneously to put the shapes in.
Pick Up Sticks®	At first, have your child grab two sticks at a time, or at least use their RIGHT hand.
Punch Art	Print different letters, numbers, or pictures without too much detail and then encourage your child to use a tack or small pin to punch on the line around the object (make sure they do this on a surface the pin can penetrate). As their fine motor skills improve, you can give them more detailed pictures.

IF YOUR CHILD IS LEFT BRAIN WEAK

ACTIVITY	SMALL MOTOR DESCRIPTION
Sandbox	Use a small plastic swimming pool filled with sand if you don't have one, and hide objects (letters, numbers, etc.) in the sand. Encourage your child to get dirty digging for them!
Sidewalk Chalk	Encourage your child to write notes to their friends or practice math on the sidewalk.
Stringing Beads	Make sure your child uses their RIGHT hand to see how many they can string together within a certain time period. Start with larger objects and progressively use smaller and smaller ones. (The slower the pace, the smaller the benefit).
Wikki Sticks®	Make sure your child follows the instructions (not their imaginations) to create something. Following the instructions to create the exact object stimulates the LEFT hemisphere.

IF YOUR CHILD IS LEFT BRAIN WEAK

IF YOUR CHILD IS RIGHT BRAIN WEAK

- **Encourage big picture and creative thinking**
  - Ex.: Tell your child a story and focus on the moral/theme, NOT the details.
  - Have your child build new Lego® creations and make up stories about what they created.
  - Work through math story problems.

- **Encourage new and different activities and experiences**
  - It is critical to give your child as many new activities and experiences as possible...new places, new faces, new books, new activities, new, new, new!
  - Change the order of their schedule, take an alternate route home, etc.
  - Everything should be as **different** as you can make it!

- **Encourage activities involving shapes**
  - Play games involving shapes (e.g., Perfection®).

- **Encourage activities involving colors**
  - Abstract art or painting.
  - When doing counting exercises use colors instead.
  - Ex.: Rather than 1, 2, 3, 4, 5...say, red, blue, green, orange, yellow.

- **Encourage creative thinking activities and games**
  - Encourage imaginary play (e.g., pretend they're pirates, etc.)
  - Ex.: Charades®, Cranium®, Balderdash®, Pictionary®, putting on a puppet show and singing songs, etc.

- **Encourage deep pressure touch**
  - Massaging, normal to rough tickling, or joint compressions, but only on the LEFT side of the body.

IF YOUR CHILD IS RIGHT BRAIN WEAK

- **Encourage exposure to low frequency sounds**
  - Ex.: Listening to lower tones and sounds and instruments like the guitar, bass, organ, or drums

- **Encourage exposure to slow paced music**
  - Ex.: Relaxing music, classical music [if not too high-pitched] or "easy-listening" music.

- **Encourage physical activity**
  - The more movement (e.g., running, jumping, playing, biking, etc.) your child engages in, the more he/she is stimulating the RIGHT brain.
  - Play Red Rover, Hide-N-Go-Seek, Freeze Tag, etc.
  - Core building activities, biking, gymnastics, rock climbing, Karate, etc.
  - Keep them moving as much as possible! It's all about the *MOTOR! MOTOR! MOTOR!*

IF YOUR CHILD IS RIGHT BRAIN WEAK

- ❑ **Avoid anything involving lots of detail**
  - Ex.: When building with Legos®, don't copy a detailed image or model.

- ❑ **Avoid anything involving numbers**
  - Sudoku®, math games, counting, card games (e.g., Uno®).
  - Don't count your child's exercises out loud.

- ❑ **Avoid any repetitive behaviors or activities**
  - Ex.: Don't read the same book more than once. Don't let your child do the same activities, talk about the same subjects, wear the same clothes, etc.

- ❑ **Avoid activities involving letters**
  - No crossword puzzles, word searches, or other word games.
  - No fact-based or educational books.
  - Reading is fine BUT your child should only read: (1) new, (2) different, and (3) imaginary or fantasy type books.
  - Reading is very sedentary, so you should only allow it for brief periods each day and then get them moving!

- ❑ **Avoid anything they are obsessed with, or gravitate towards**
  - Avoid things that your child is naturally good at (and wants to do) as much as possible. (This will be difficult because they are things they like and enjoy doing).
  - Don't let your child play with the same toys, read about the same subjects, talk about the same things, etc.

- ❑ **Avoid being too planned or scheduled**
  - Ex.: Don't follow a rigorous schedule, or plan out your child's days, weeks, or months.

- ❑ **Avoid memory games or memorizing**
  - Ex.: Don't play Memory Match®, use flash cards, memorize facts, details, books, or stories.

IF YOUR CHILD IS RIGHT BRAIN WEAK

- ❏ **Avoid linear or logical thinking or activities**
  - Ex.: Don't play chess, checkers, or analytical games.

- ❏ **Avoid light touch or soft tickling**

- ❏ **Avoid high frequency sounds**
  - No high-pitched sounds and instruments such as the violin, flute, etc.

- ❏ **Avoid fast paced music**
  - No fast music or rock and roll, especially if it's high pitched.
  - No music with lots of words.

- ❏ **Avoid excessive screen time and exposure to technology**
  - Technology is particularly addictive for the left hemisphere.
  - Reduce screen time (including computer, video games, iPads, iPhones, etc.) during weekdays to 1 hour and to 2 hours on weekends.

- ❏ **Avoid sedentary play or any activity that involves sitting for extended periods of time**
  - Make sure that drawing, reading, relaxing, Legos®, Playdough®, or art projects don't last longer than 20 minutes at a time.
  - Do your best to limit sedentary play to 1 hour per day.

IF YOUR CHILD IS RIGHT BRAIN WEAK

ACTIVITY	LARGE MOTOR DESCRIPTION
Badminton	Improves hand-eye coordination. Make sure your child remains active during the game and don't keep score!
Baseball	Improves hand-eye coordination. Change the batting order each time, make everyone run the bases in between each batter, and don't keep score!
Basketball	Play full court to increase running and movement. If possible, lower the basket for easier shooting. Make everyone do laps around the court after each basket and don't keep score!
Bikes/Scooters	Start out slow (with training wheels if needed) and take a new route or path each time. Eventually, build up to going faster, doing hills, etc.
Bean Bag Toss	Start close and then move farther back each time. You can also toss it back and forth to each other as well.
Bounce House	Great for jumping, bouncing, and the cross-crawl motion of climbing up the ladders, etc. Just keep your child moving!
Bowling	Make sure the ball isn't too heavy for your child. Demonstrate the proper form and where to aim. Bowl with bumpers to help them be more successful and don't keep score!
Camping	Exposes your child to new environments and experiences. Go on hikes and sing campfire songs. Encourage your child to take special notice of trees, animals, and the beautiful surroundings.
Croquet	Improves hand-eye coordination. Make sure your child remains active during the game and don't keep score!
Dancing	Put on the music and just have a good time. Encourage big muscle movements. Teach your child steps involving rhythm and timing, but don't have them memorize routines.
Dodgeball	Use a larger ball to make it easier to catch. Instruct your child not to throw too hard or at the face. Make sure they stay active during the game.
Fishing	Always fish in a different spot. Instruct your child on proper techniques and while waiting for the fish to bite, tell each other creative stories.

IF YOUR CHILD IS RIGHT BRAIN WEAK

ACTIVITY	LARGE MOTOR DESCRIPTION
Flag Football	Make sure it isn't overly rough. If your child has difficulty catching the ball, hand it off instead and get them running! Just have fun and don't keep score!
Frisbee	Keep your child moving and running to make the catch. But, if catching the frisbee is too difficult, just throw it towards them and have them try to dodge it instead.
Golf	Mini- or regular golf, go to the driving range, or even just hit balls in a field. If you take your child to a course, don't use a cart.
Gymnastics	Improves balance and core strength! Your child can do this at home, or you can enroll them in classes!
Hiking/Climbing	Indoor/outdoor hikes that accommodate your child's endurance level before consistently increasing the intensity over time.
Hockey	Use rollerblades if possible and play with taped brooms and balls in the street and remember not to keep score.
Hokey Pokey	Use exaggerated movements and complete the steps in a different order each time!
Hoola Hoop®	Encourage your child to spin it around their arm, leg, waist, or neck...or just have them roll it on the ground without letting the hoop fall over.
Hopscotch	Indoor/outdoor hopscotch with tape/chalk as appropriate but use colors instead of numbers.
Horseback Riding	Improves core strength and balance.
Hot Potato	Stand in a circle and pass around a different object each round (e.g., a ball, a toy, a potato, a pillow, etc.) Play the appropriate music and when it stops, whoever is holding the object is out.
Ice Blocking	Buy a large block of ice, fold up a towel and place it on the block. Find a grassy large hill (a different one each time) and encourage your child to sit on the block to slide down the hill. Make sure they push their own ice block back up the hill each time.

IF YOUR CHILD IS RIGHT BRAIN WEAK

ACTIVITY	LARGE MOTOR DESCRIPTION
Ice Skating	Hold on tightly to your child if they have difficulty with balance and just be patient until their balance improves. ☺
Jump Rope	Set the rope on the ground and have the person at each end make it wiggle like a snake while your child jumps over it. Work up to having them jump rope on their own by having two people turn the rope as they jump…or tie one side to a doorknob while you hold the other.
Karate	Builds discipline, self-esteem, physical movement, and coordination. Make sure your child is able to follow directions and sit still before attempting this since most dojos don't allow kids to run around.
Kayaking	Be careful (wear a life jacket) and make sure your child helps you paddle.
Kickball	If your child has difficulty kicking the ball while it's rolling, place it in front of them instead. Make sure they run the bases as fast at they can and don't keep score!
Laser Tag	Make sure your child remains active during the game and encourage them to imagine they're different characters each round.
Obstacle Course	Indoor/outdoor using pillows, blankets, chairs, tables, etc. Encourage your child to help you create different courses and time how fast they complete it.
Paint Ball	Be careful! ☺
Parks	Go to a different park each time and continue rotating. Keep your child moving and playing with only short breaks. Encourage them to use their imagination (e.g., they're on a desert island, in outer space, etc.)
Playing Catch	Start with a bigger ball and stand closer together until your child becomes comfortable being farther away.
Potato Sack Race	Use pillowcases for the race and encourage your child to run hard enough to get good exercise.

IF YOUR CHILD IS RIGHT BRAIN WEAK

ACTIVITY	LARGE MOTOR DESCRIPTION
Red Rover	Keep it fun! If your child becomes frustrated from being unable to break through, make sure someone lets them through. Increase the activity level by having them run laps between each turn.
Relay Races	Encourage your child to use their imagination by combining different activities with the race (e.g., skipping part of the way, hopping, etc.).
Ring Around the Rosies	Encourage your child to spin clockwise.
Ring Toss	If your child struggles with this activity, encourage them to start closer so they can be successful and don't keep score.
Running/ Jogging	Make sure to frequently change the route and build your child's endurance over time.
Skiing/ Snow-boarding	Improves core strength and balance.
Slip n' Slide®	Use the Slip n' Slide® (or a long role of painters' plastic) in your backyard or nearby grassy hill.
Soccer	Ignore the rules and don't keep score. Run back and forth trying to kick the ball into the net (regardless of which side)! Your child can also practice kicking the ball back and forth but encourage them to use their left foot more often.
Sock Snowball Fights	Use rolled up socks for "snowballs" and then run, jump, duck, and dodge!
Stair Climbing	Encourage your child to run up and down stairs. Make it a relay race by placing something at the top of the stairs to grab and pass on to the next runner. If you don't have stairs, just have your child run in place, or march around the house while singing songs.
Swimming	If possible, rotate the pools you go to and have your child work on their swimming strokes instead of just splashing around. Play Marco Polo®, pretend to be in the ocean, etc.

IF YOUR CHILD IS RIGHT BRAIN WEAK

ACTIVITY	LARGE MOTOR DESCRIPTION
T-ball	Improves hand-eye coordination and is great for kids who aren't ready for baseball yet. Make sure your child runs the bases as fast as they can!
Tennis	Improves motor movements, hand-eye coordination, rhythm, and timing, BUT make sure your child is ready for this because it can be challenging to simultaneously move and hit the ball. Start with having them hit the ball against the wall or bounce it on the racquet before progressing to playing the game.
Trampoline	Encourage your child to try different simple tricks or even take them to trampoline arenas and bounce houses.
Volleyball	Improves hand-eye coordination.
Walking	Start with short walks and gradually increase the distance each time until your child's endurance improves.
Water Fights	Water balloon volleyball is really fun! Have two kids hold each end of a towel and place a water balloon on it. Toss it over the net to other players or toss it up and down while trying to catch it on the towel. Have them around the yard and throw water balloons or wet sponges at each other.
Waterskiing Wakeboarding Kneeboarding Tubing	Improves balance and is a great workout (and lots of fun)!
Weightlifting	Start with light weights and increase the amount each time until your child's strength improves.
Wrestling	Basic wrestling and roughhousing is great fun and exercise but be careful! ☺
Yoga	Learn some basic children's yoga (check YouTube®) and then practice it often with your child. Make sure they perform their deep breathing exercises.

IF YOUR CHILD IS RIGHT BRAIN WEAK

ACTIVITY	SMALL MOTOR DESCRIPTION
Clay/Dough	Gluten-free only (Play-Dough® brand is not). Your child should be creating something new and different each time.
Coloring	Encourage your child to color more abstract objects, patterns, or shapes and work on staying in the lines. Remember to frequently switch to different pictures and types of pictures.
Crochet	Excellent for developing fine motor skills. It encourages synchronization because your child is simultaneously using both hands.
Cross Stitch	Great for fine motor and for synchronization because they are simultaneously using both hands.
Finger Painting	Excellent for developing fine motor and tactile skills. Encourage your child to paint on big posters, old T-shirts, or even with their toes!
Lacing Cards	Make sure your child doesn't do the same cards over and over…and that they use their LEFT hand.
Moonsand/ Moondough	Great for fine motor and tactile skills. Encourage your child to create something different each time and to tell you a story about it. (It's also great imaginary play!)
Operation®	Assess your child's level of ability and if necessary…turn off the buzzer to prevent frustration…allow them to use the tweezers to grab the objects…time them to see how fast they can collect all the objects (speed helps develop fine motor).
Painting	Excellent for developing creativity and fine motor skills. Encourage your child to paint something as simple as watercolors or water books…or more advanced like enrolling in art classes, etc.
Perfection®	Excellent for developing fine motor skills and speed. Start by having your child only use their LEFT hand during the game. To improve synchronization, place a pile of disks on either side of them and make sure they use both hands simultaneously to put the shapes in.
Pick Up Sticks®	At first, have your child grab two sticks at a time, or at least use their LEFT hand.

IF YOUR CHILD IS RIGHT BRAIN WEAK

ACTIVITY	SMALL MOTOR DESCRIPTION
Punch Art	Print different letters, numbers, or pictures without too much detail and then encourage your child use a tack or small pin to punch on the line around the object (make sure they do this on a surface the pin can penetrate). As their fine motor skills improve, you can give them more detailed pictures.
Sandbox	Use a small plastic swimming pool filled with sand if you don't have one, and encourage your child to build sandcastles, play, and just generally get dirty!
Sidewalk Chalk	Encourage your child to create and draw different pictures each time.
Stringing Beads	Make sure your child uses their LEFT hand to see how many they can string together within a certain time period. Start with larger objects and progressively use smaller ones. (The slower the pace, the smaller the benefit).
Wikki Sticks®	Make sure your child doesn't follow the directions, but instead uses their own imagination and creativity to make something.

IF YOUR CHILD IS RIGHT BRAIN WEAK

APPENDIX Nº5
THE RESOURCE GUIDE

Resources that inform, inspire, encourage, and empower you to help your children become the best version of themselves.

THE RESOURCE GUIDE

Autism: The scientific truth about preventing, diagnosing, and treating autism spectrum disorders—and what parents can do now
BY DR. ROBERT MELILLO

Disconnected Kids: The ground-breaking Brain Balance® program for children with autism, ADHD, dyslexia, and other neurological disorders
BY DR. ROBERT MELILLO

Reconnected Kids: Help your children achieve physical, mental, and emotional balance
BY DR. ROBERT MELILLO

THE RESOURCE GUIDE

The Disconnected Kids Nutrition Plan: Proven strategies to enhance learning and focus for children with autism, ADHD, dyslexia, and other neurological disorders
BY DR. ROBERT MELILLO

Overcoming Dyslexia: A new and complete science-based program for reading problems at any level
BY SALLY SHAYWITZ, M.D.

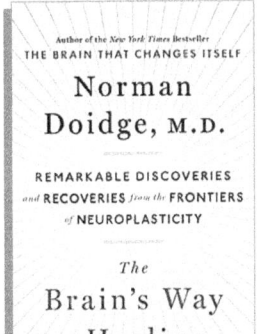

The Brain's Way of Healing: Remarkable discoveries and recoveries from the frontiers of neuroplasticity
BY NORMAIN DOIDGE, M.D.

THE RESOURCE GUIDE

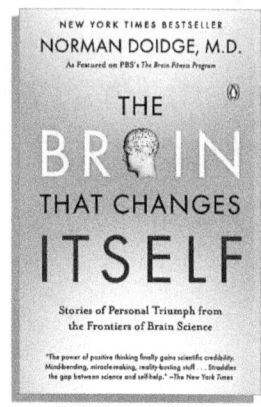

The Brain That Changes Itself: Stories of personal triumph from the frontiers of science
BY NORMAN DOIDGE, M.D.

Soft-Wired: How the new science of brain plasticity can change your life
BY DR. MICHAEL MERZENICH, Ph.D.

Kids Beyond Limits: Breakthrough results for children with autism, Asperger's, brain damage, ADHD, and undiagnosed developmental delays
BY ANAT BANIEL

THE RESOURCE GUIDE

Why Gender Matters: What parents and teachers need to know about the emerging science of sex differences
BY LEONARD SAX, M.D., Ph.D.

Boys Adrift: The five factors driving the growing epidemic of unmotivated boys and underachieving young men
BY LEONARD SAX, M.D., Ph.D.

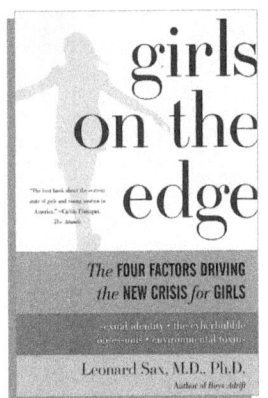

Girls on the Edge: The four factors driving the new crisis for girls — sexual identity, the cyberbubble, obsessions, environmental toxins
BY LEONARD SAX, M.D., Ph.D.

THE RESOURCE GUIDE

The Perfect YOU: A blueprint for identity
BY DR. CAROLINE LEAF

Finding Your Element: How to discover your talents and passions and transform your life
BY KEN ROBINSON

Grooming the Next Generation for Success: Proven strategies for raising the next generation of leaders
BY DANI JOHNSON

Preparing Kids for LIFE

life = education without walls

www.PK4L.com

www.ingramcontent.com/pod-product-compliance
Lightning Source LLC
Chambersburg PA
CBHW060457300426
44113CB00016B/2618